Harvesting the Wild

gathering and using food from nature

A self-reliance guide from Backwoods Home Magazine

Contributors —

Jackie Clay, Eugene Mitchell, Linda Gabris, Ben Crookshanks, Alice Brantley Yeager, James O. Yeager, Rick Brannan, Cynthia Andal, Devon Winter

ISBN 978-0-9821577-7-0
Copyright 1997-2009

Backwoods Home Magazine
PO Box 712
Gold Beach, Oregon 97444
www.backwoodshome.com

Edited by Ilene Duffy, Rhoda Denning, Lisa Nourse
Cover design by Annie Tuttle

Contents

Foraging wild foods is good for you	5
Harvesting the wild: Greens	9
Clover: from livestock forage to medicinal tea, this humble plant is one of nature's best gifts	22
Stinging Nettle: Mother Nature's healthiest pick	29
Harvesting the wild: Asparagus	37
Harvesting the wild: Flower buds	47
Wild raspberries: Summertime's finest treat	52
Harvesting the wild: Blueberries	57
Ramps: Better than garlic breath	71
Wild garlic: Independent & delicious	76
Plantain	81
Harvesting the wild: Cactus	86
Birch tree syrup	97
Harvesting the wild: Acorns	100
Harvesting the wild: Hazelnuts	111
The enchanting Chanterelle: Gourmet goodies free from the forest	113
Harvesting the wild: Shaggy mane mushrooms	123
Wonderful wilderness wines	127
Wonderful wilderness teas	134

A self-reliance guide from Backwoods Home Magazine

Foraging wild foods is good for you

By Jackie Clay

When I was a kid, one of my favorite times was late in the autumn, when the whole family (including the dogs) would pile into Dad's well-used station wagon and we'd drive for miles out through country lanes, searching for wild nuts. I can see those half-bare trees now, silhouetted against sunny skies: black walnut, shagbark hickory, butternut, and hazelnut. All fair game for us Rheads.

Packing a picnic lunch, baskets for nut-gathering, and burlap sacks to hold our bounty, we joyously thrashed the fallen leaves along roadsides, pouncing on what seemed like hundreds of pounds of nuts. It was like an Easter hunt, only I always did like nuts better than candy. What a surprise it was, when I grew older, to find out that I actually *liked* something that was good for me.

Come to think of it, foraging wild foods is pretty darned good for you, in a whole lot of ways. Some you would scarcely imagine.

Wild foods are totally organically grown, contain no toxic pesticides, fertilizers, or herbicides.

Did you ever think of how many man-induced chemicals are in most foods you buy at the grocery store? Not to be a killjoy, but consider the spray to kill the weeds in the fields before the seeds or plants are planted, the chemical fertilizer used to make it grow quickly, the spray to keep it "bug-free," the fumigation to keep it from ripening too quickly or from sprouting during shipment or storage.

With wild foods (with the exception of those gathered from agricultural land, of course), there is absolutely *none* of this. My wild chokecherries have no "bugs" or worms, but are never sprayed with anything but a good rain. My wild greens only contain natural nutrients. Our wild-foraged roots are not dipped or sprayed to prevent sprouting. These wild foods are, in the truest sense of the word, pure.

Wild foods contain many vitamins, minerals, and other nutrients vital to healthy living.

When man was a hunter/gatherer by necessity, he had not yet "discovered" nutrition. But by instinct or God-given inner knowledge, he managed a diet to keep him and his family well. Now modern man must take bottles of supplements to even function on a "normal" level. Why is that, you may wonder? Maybe because we are too good to eat "lowly weeds," which contain more nutrition than do hothouse forced vegetables and out-of-season tasteless fruits—and none of the chemicals.

Take, for instance, a common garden weed called lamb's quarters. Could you imagine that it contains high amounts of vitamins A and C, thiamine, riboflavin, niacin, and amino acids? And to top it off, it actually *tastes* great too.

Most all wild-gathered grains, greens, roots, fruits, and vegetables stack up very well in the nutrition department.

And wild foods grow just about everywhere, with no (or in spite of?) cultivation.

One very striking example of how the lack of wild-foraged diet has injured the health of a group of people is shown by a study done on the Pima and other Native American Indian and Hispanic peoples of the U.S-Mexico border area. In the not-so-distant past, these people relied on native foods for nearly all of their diet. Homegrown corn, beans and other traditional vegetables were supplemented greatly by wild foraged foods, such as prickly pear and other cactus, mesquite pod flour, etc.

After World War II this changed. Enter white flour, grease, and "convenience" foods. Formerly healthy people, they began experiencing obesity, high cholesterol levels, and diabetes. The abandoned "old, dirty" foods were high in fiber and high in nutrition; the new modern foods were high in empty calories, fat, and sugar.

The good news is that with an effort to return to the old ways of gathering and growing food, this can be—and has in many cases been—reversed. For more information, contact Native Seeds/SEARCH, 526 N. Fourth Ave., Tucson, AZ 85705 (Web Site: www.nativeseeds.org) They also have a seed catalog with many native and traditional varieties of vegetable, herb, and other great seed, many of which we grow and recommend ourselves.

Wild foraging is good exercise. (Exercise that is not boring.)

You can do 50 sit-ups, jog two miles, and do boring exercises *or* you can spend the day hiking country lanes, mountainsides, and creek bottoms gathering tasty, nutritious wild foods. Your choice. I guarantee, you'll get bending, stretching, gentle lifting, walking up and down hills, plus plenty of good fresh air each time you go.

And the more wild foods you hunt, the more varied the landscape you'll traverse, from wild lakesides, gathering wild rice, cattails, and duck potatoes to dramatic arid desert valleys where you'll forage cactus, yucca, mesquite pods, and chiltipines (wild peppers). Actually, it's so much fun, you may find you switch "vacation" for foraging wild foods. Our family would be bored to tears in Disneyland. We may hike 11 miles gathering wild foods, getting plenty of good, gentle exercise. But we may see a moose foraging pond lilies, two eagles tumbling over and over in a territorial dispute, or surprise a new fawn in a creekside glen to boot.

Foraging wild foods is good to alleviate depression.

In addition to the beneficial exercise your body gets, your spirits get a great boost, just getting out and looking for those tasty wild treats. It matters little what you end up gathering, rather that you go and look.

Many is the time we went out for wild raspberries and came back with something entirely different—perhaps a sack of greens to home can, a basket of mushrooms, or just a few foods and a lot of smiles. My late husband, Bob, suffered from PTSD (Post Traumatic Stress Disorder) from a couple tours in Vietnam. And I can tell you that a good hike in the hills foraging wild foods did more to help him than did anything else. There's a lot to be said for "getting back to nature." Stress, worry, anger, and fear just kind of melt.

You can go out with your family or alone, if you prefer, and have a great day seeing all the little (and grand) things nature has to offer. You harvest nutritious and very tasty foods you can eat fresh or put up for later use. Coming home, a bit tired, but somehow renewed, you realize humans were created to gather wild foods. God didn't give Adam and Eve a convenience store. He gave them the Garden of Eden. And when we slip into convenience store type living it injures our whole being.

So instead of sitting for hours in front of a television set that numbs your mind and disgusts your soul, or reading the newspaper, which only has "bad" news, how about giving wild foraging a try? It's the best "medicine" for your whole being. And it doesn't cost a cent. Do it regularly. Take your family along. It builds togetherness, confidence, and a sense of greater self-reliance.

Foraging wild foods is *not* just for "survival" situations, it's for *healthy* living. ∆

Harvesting the wild: Greens

By Jackie Clay

Winter's dreary end seems to drag on and on into early spring. We itch to get planting the garden, poring over seed catalogs and babying those tiny light green tomato, pepper, and other infant plants in the south windows. How lucky we are that the very first delectable greens that our bodies crave are already growing in sunny, protected areas around the homestead, planted for us by God, himself.

More than a few mothers have taken a basket and paring knife, desperately scrounging around the south sides of buildings, trying to find enough tender, nourishing greens to feed their family during hard times. This was especially common during pioneer years and during the lean Great Depression. Such common "weeds" as dandelion, purslane, pig weed, and lamb's quarter are very nourishing. And they are extremely tasty, to boot.

Each year, our family forages for and harvests many local wild greens to enjoy with simple meals. And we like them so much that I can and dry several varieties to use year-around. One benefit of eating "weeds" is that they grow exceedingly well, as we all know from weeding the lawn and garden. While we struggle to get that row of spinach to grow during warm weather, the pigweed and lambs quarters simply shoot up.

(Did you know that no one can tell my home-canned spinach from these weeds when canned, as well?)

Let's take a look at some of the more common and easily identified wild greens. Of course, as with any wild foraging, we must be sure of the plants we pick as there are some poisonous little buggers out there that we sure don't want to serve for dinner. And take care not to harvest any plants from an area that might have been sprayed with insecticides, chemical fertilizers, or orchard sprays.

Pigweed (wild amaranth)

The coarse, lowly pigweed is one of our most favorite wild greens. Most folks call pigweed a blankety-blank weed. But they've never actually cooked up a mess or they would realize what a jewel they have clogging up the garden rows. When we first looked on our New Mexico homestead, walking over the abandoned cow yard with shoulder-high pigweed and waist-high lambs quarter among other edible wild plants, I thought to myself, "Well, here we could never starve to death!"

The most common pigweed is the red-rooted pigweed. It is a coarse weed—even when young—vigorous and quick growing. The leaves are oval and come to a point, with distinct ribs and wavy or scalloped edges. The leaves grow in a widely branched rosette, with the new growth tighter and held above the older leaves. The leaf stems are a pale greenish pink, and the root a distinct red. You will seldom find only one pigweed; it is a prolific reseeder. This fact makes it a nasty garden weed, but ensures that it is also an abundant vegetable. (One plant can have more than 100,000 seeds.)

This fact is also important, as the seeds are not only edible, but very good. Pigweed is wild amaranth which is an important food to many Native Peoples all across North and South America.

Pigweed is nutritious in all forms, being high in vitamins A and C and high in iron and calcium. There is one caution. In farmland and in some Western American areas, pigweed can store up dangerous amounts of nitrates. This does not mean you should not eat pigweed. Be moderate, varying it with other forms of greens.

We begin to pick pigweed when it is about six inches tall and very tender, continuing the harvest through summer when the plants shoot up. With larger plants, harvest only the tender leaves and stems, including the growing rosette at the top. Once it begins to flower, we either pull the plant or cut off the top to encourage new growth. The main stem and larger side stems become woody and inedible, as do sunflowers. (The stems of our New Mexican cow yard pigweeds became so large that we literally had to cut them with a chain saw.)

Cooking pigweed is simple. The most common use is to simply rinse the leaves and steam or boil until wilted and tender. A dab of butter and a sprinkle of salt and vinegar and you have real good eating.

You can substitute pigweed greens for any recipe calling for spinach. The raw leaves are a bit rough, so if you use the most tender leaves in salads, you probably will choose to add only a few until you see how your family likes the mixture.

One of our favorite recipes for pigweed is piggy quiche, your basic spinach quiche, only using abundant and tasty pigweed.

Piggy quiche:

1 unbaked flaky pie crust
6 large eggs, separated
¼ cup mushrooms
1 red bell pepper, sliced
½ tsp. salt
pinch rubbed sage
1 tsp. butter

1 cup slightly wilted pigweed leaves & tender stems
1 small onion, chopped
½ cup grated sharp cheddar cheese
¼ tsp. Tabasco sauce
½ tsp. roasted, mashed garlic (optional)

Rub unbaked pie crust with butter. Whip egg whites until stiff, then fold in the beaten egg yolks. Mix gently. In saucepan, sauteé chopped onion, sliced mushrooms, and green pepper until barely tender. Mix in slightly steam-wilted pigweed leaves and tender stems. Add seasonings and cheese to egg. Mix gently. Add vegetables. Pour into pie crust. Bake at 375° F until a toothpick inserted in the center comes out clean. Serve at once. This simple quiche can be put together, including making the pie crust, in half an hour and tastes like it took all day. (Never tell 'em they're eating weeds.)

The seeds of the pigweed are very good. In fact, amaranth is very well known, especially south of the border, as a grain. There are many varieties of domestic edible amaranth available, bred especially for their tasty seed production. As I've said, an amaranth plant can produce more than 100,000 seeds. And all of them are tasty.

To gather the seeds, wait until the plants mature and die in the fall, turning brown and brittle. Then, before the wind sows billions of potential weed seeds right in your garden, gently clip the seed heads off into a paper bag such as an empty feed sack that is clean. Do this on a dry day when the plants are quite dry to avoid mold problems during curing. Fill the sack with seed heads, but do not pack them down, allowing for air circulation. Store the sack in a warm, dry area, protected from birds and rodents. In about a week, the seeds will shatter out quite easily.

I tie the sack shut with stout twine, then simply walk on the bag quite briskly, even stomping gently on it. Turn the bag over and repeat. Shake the bag. You'll begin to hear lots of little seeds rattling happily in the bottom. Repeat again, until you think you've threshed the seeds out pretty well. Then untie the twine and gently pull out one seed head over a newspaper. Examine it, rubbing the hulls between your fingers. I'd recommend wearing gloves as amaranth seed heads are picky. More than one Indian tribe refers to pigweed as "that which picks the fingers."

When the seeds have been mostly threshed free, I pour the sack's contents a little at a time into a screen or basket with smaller holes between weaves, held over a large, clean, dry container such as a canning kettle.

Harvesting the Wild—gathering and using food from nature

Shake the sieve and watch the little seeds trickle through into the kettle.

Throw the spent heads into another paper sack to burn, as there are always some seeds that never thresh out and you sure don't want to add them to your compost pile.

Now you have a kettle with a good layer of tiny seeds mixed with chaff. On a fairly windy day, winnow out the chaff by simply pouring the seeds from one container to another on the ground, with a foot or so between them. The wind will carry the light chaff away, and let the heavier seeds fall to the lower container. **Do not** do this in a heavy wind, as amaranth seeds are small and fairly light and will blow away in a stout wind.

You may now toast the seeds by spreading thinly on a cookie sheet in an oven set at 250° F and baking for about 15 minutes, stirring occasionally to prevent scorching. Toasting gives the grain a nutty flavor.

The raw or toasted seeds may now be ground with a mortar and pestle or blender and added to any multi-grain bread. To each five cups of wheat flour, you can add a cup of amaranth flour.

Or you can make a traditional "mush" by simmering 1 cup of water with 1 cup of ground amaranth seeds. The toasted seeds work best for this unusual breakfast food. Adding dried fruit improves the flavor to those accustomed to more zesty fare.

Lamb's quarters

Another wild green that is a favorite of ours is lamb's quarters. Also a common garden weed, plentiful in most areas of the country, this wild vegetable is easily gathered in the spring and early summer. In some parts of the country, lamb's quarter is called pigweed, but is not a true pigweed or amaranth, but a chenopodium.

Lamb's quarters has triangular, notched leaves that look sort of like a goose's foot. This is why, in some parts of the country, folks call it "goosefoot."

The veins of the leaves are whitish, and the undersides and tops of new leaves are sparkling with white "fairy dust." We pick lamb's quarters when it is about eight inches to a foot tall. When it gets too large, the stems become woody and tough.

Lamb's quarter's leaves are quite good in a salad or just for a snack on cool mornings with dew still clinging to them.

Like pigweed, however, don't go overboard eating this green exclusively, as it can harbor nitrates in heavily farmed and fertilized areas. And lamb's quarter contains oxalic acid, which can be harmful when consumed in bulk over quite a lengthy period.

Common lamb's quarter is easy to spot with its scalloped oval and pointed leaves. Pick when young and tender.

But when eaten in moderation, as one would any garden vegetable, there is scarcely any better green, domestic or wild. We use a lot of it, off and on, all year, for I home can pints and pints of lamb's quarter to use during the winter.

Besides being very tasty, the lamb's quarter is extremely nutritious, being high in vitamins A, C, riboflavin, thiamine, and niacin. It's easy to see why this green was a staple of many ancient cultures, from Europe to North and South America.

While we were in New Mexico, many of our Spanish neighbors carried burlap feed sacks into pastures and abandoned homesteads to pick "quelites" or "greens," namely the succulent lamb's quarters. And we were right there with them with our own sacks. Then the next day, the greens were rinsed, boiled in salt water just enough to wilt them, and packed into canning jars and processed to ensure that we had enough lamb's quarters to last until the next spring's crop was abundant.

One of my favorite recipes for lamb's quarters is to fry a slice of ham, then add a tablespoon of butter to the frying pan when the ham has been removed. Then sprinkle handfuls of fresh, rinsed lamb's quarter into the pan, stir-frying until just wilted and tender. Sometimes I add a small chopped onion or mellow mild red chile pepper, which has been seeded. Served hot, along with the fried ham, you have a pretty darned good lunch. (For those of you who do not eat pork, a slice of smoked venison ham works equally well.)

Like pigweed, the seeds of lamb's quarter are also tasty. They are tiny, but we find they thrash out quite easily, just as do those for pigweed seed. You may toast the seeds and/or grind them to make mush or flour. It's fun to add wild seed ground grain to your homemade breads. Try sprinkling toasted lamb's quarter seeds on the tops of buttered, baked rolls and bread as you would poppy or sesame seeds. Pretty darned good.

Dandelion

The dandelion is one weed which needs little introduction. Many of us grew up digging this tenacious weed out of our folks' lawns and gardens. With its cheery bright yellow flower, we think it's as pretty in our lawn as planted crocus and daffodils. And at the Clay homestead, it is very seldom ever pulled as a weed.

The dandelion is very nutritious, perhaps *the* most nutritious garden vegetable. Pretty darned impressive for a weed. It is very high in vitamins A, B1, B2, B3, C, D, and many minerals, such as calcium, zinc, selenium, magnesium, iron, manganese, phosphorous, potassium, and sodium.

Nearly every part of the plant is not only edible, but delectable, and different tasting than the others. The flowers, twisted and pinched off the stems, are sweet and when steamed just enough to make them less "fuzzy" to the mouth, they are wonderful drizzled with butter and sprinkled with vinegar and salt.

The leaves are a bit bitter but still very good, both raw and cooked. The steamed or boiled leaves are more mild than the raw ones, and when more bitter leaves are boiled in two waters they become milder. Never over-boil dandelion or it loses its health benefits.

The crown, or smaller rosette of leaves, and small, unopened buds just at and barely below ground level are like a separate vegetable, being mild and succulent to the taste.

Even the slender, parsnip-like root of the dandelion is good to eat. I scrub the larger roots well with a pot scrubber, then lay them in a shallow baking dish. If the root seems woody or stringy, I scrape or peel it, depending on the root. Then bake the roots in a moderate oven until tender. Serve with a dab of butter or chill and add to cold salads.

You can even toast the roots in an oven with the very lowest temperature or with only the pilot light on until crisp, but not scorched. Then run through a grinder or your blender. Now you have a coffee substitute which can be brewed just as you would coffee. (I hate coffee and think roasted dandelion root tastes *much* better.) This could come in handy as a survival drink for those of you who just need that morning cup of java. Unfortunately, you won't get a caffeine fix, as dandelion is caffeine-free.

One problem for many people is that the dandelion grows so low to the ground that it is often gritty with blown dirt. This makes it hard to rinse clean enough to get the grit out completely. I find that a salad spinner does a great job. Or lacking that tool, rinsing the plant vigorously, under strong running water, will do quite a good job.

Cattail

Nearly everyone is familiar with the cattail, especially its round, cigar-shaped fuzzy seedheads. Besides being fun to whack each other with (as kids we would watch the fuzzy seeds blow about in the wind), the cattail plant is a storehouse of good eating. From the very top (the yellow pollen), to the mucky bottom (fleshy roots), the cattail provides a wide variety of edibles for the wild forager. And you don't have to get very "wild," either, as the cattail is common in farm ponds, along streams, and in lowlands nationwide.

Do not pick cattails from polluted bodies of water, or those having high-nitrate run-off from farm fields. Also be careful about harvesting from heavy traffic areas, due to auto pollutants.

Be sure of the plant you pick, because the wild flag, or wild iris, which has a blue-purple flower is toxic to consume, lives in the same habitat as the cattail, and has quite similar leaves. Generally, the cattail leaves are wider and more hollow. The wild flag's leaves are iris-like and flat down to the bottom, where the cattail shoot is rounded right down to the root.

Like many other wild foods, the cattail is extremely nutritious in all forms.

Our first spring foraging trips always include a side trip to a remote mountain marshy creek, where abundant cattails grow. As a child canoeing with my parents, we would pull tender white cattail shoots from the water to eat as a snack on each trip. These taste just like a mild cucumber. Simply grasp the green cattail leaves of young plants and pull upward. The shoot comes up easily, with the lower portion being a very succulent, tender white.

Dip these in your favorite vegetable dip or simply sprinkle with vinegar dressing as you would a garden cucumber, and you have a wild salad deluxe. I've even made wild pickles by using sliced cattail shoots in place of cucumbers for fresh refrigerator pickles, from dill to bread and butter types.

This same blanched, tender shoot can be steamed for ten minutes and served with butter or a cream sauce and you have a tasty vegetable that tastes kind of like mild parsnips.

Likewise, in the spring for a short period of time, the spike on top of the plant above the more familiar green "hot dog" that later becomes the brown seed head, can be eaten for a delectable treat. This is sometimes called cattail corn on the cob. Like corn on the cob, you prepare it by dropping it in boiling water for about five minutes. If not tender at this point, simply let it sit in the boiled water for five or ten more minutes until it is. Then dribble butter over the spikes and sprinkle with salt and you have an excellent vegetable.

This male spike quickly goes from green (corn on the cob) to yellow. This yellow powder is the pollen, and once the spike loses its green color, it is no longer good as corn on the cob. But this yellow pollen is quite easily collected and is a flour substitute (use about half domestic flour and half pollen). To collect the pollen, simply stick the pollen spike into a paper sack and shake or beat the head inside to release the pollen.

You will get quite a bit of chaff as well, but this can be sifted out with a common flour sifter or fine screen. Once you have sifted your pollen, it is ready to use as flour. We often make pancakes or cornbread using cattail pollen, especially when out camping. It is a bit slow to absorb water, so you need to make your batter, then let it rest for half an hour, stirring occasionally, until all is evenly moist.

And finally, the root can be dug to eat as a starchy flour substitute. This is a messy job, as you can't simply pull the cattail plant. You need to get down and dirty. We wade barefoot in cattail marshes, digging down around the base of the cattail with bare toes and a pointed digging stick. The toes locate the rhizomes and the digging stick helps pry them out of their mucky bed.

Once cleaned, the rhizomes can be slowly roasted until dry. Then grind the roots between two smooth large stones to release the starchy powder. These roots contain a net of fibers, which can be picked out and the flour sifted. This flour is good to add to stews and soups or to add to your bread or pancakes. As well, they really aren't too bad roasted and eaten with salt and butter, mashed with your fork or fingers, and the good part sucked off the fiber.

Not bad at all, for this common weed of marshy places.

Purslane

Our 12-year-old son David's very favorite wild plant is purslane. This is a very common garden weed and grows nearly everywhere including waste land. This is a portulaca, related to the garden flower, and is easily recognized. It is low-growing, forming a large mat. The leaves and stems are succulent and fleshy. They are smooth and reddish in color, with the stems being more highly colored than the greenish oval leaves, which, like the garden flower, are broader at the tip than the stem end.

The plant is easy to pull, having small roots for such a hearty plant. We like purslane so much that we scarcely ever pull it from the garden.

And it is very nutritious, more so than most domestic vegetables. It is high in vitamin A, C, E, folic acid, and contains fatty acids, sterols, calcium, potassium, iron, and magnesium, to name only a few nutrients.

Besides, it is very tasty. David often just plucks leaves and stems to snack on as he weeds the garden. He calls it "my weed," and rejoices when the young plants dot the garden paths in the late spring.

After it is thoroughly rinsed, I snip up tender stems and leaves, adding it to garden salads. Or you can simply drop large pieces into boiling water for a few minutes and serve with a bit of butter or drizzled with herb vinegar. I also often stir-fry it with a little smoked meat. Or dip hand-sized pieces of purslane in deep frying batter and fry until golden brown.

The tiny black seeds can be harvested in the late summer and ground up to add to breads. The numerous seeds do take awhile to gather. (One reason hunter-gatherers were seldom over-weight.)

Home canning wild greens

These wild greens, with the exception of the cattail, can be easily home-canned, allowing us to enjoy them year-round. In fact, I generally can more wild greens than domestic greens. Not only do the wild cousins out-produce their domestic brothers—which can be finicky to grow some years—but they just plain taste better.

Wild greens **must be canned under pressure**, as they are low-acid vegetables. It is not safe to can them in a water bath canner, as they require a higher temperature to kill possible harmful bacteria. But this is easy to do using a pressure canner.

Simply harvest and rinse your wild greens well to get rid of all grit and dirt. Pick through them, discarding any insect-chewed leaves or dry leaves. Then dip them into a large pot of boiling water for just long enough to wilt them. A large amount of greens will wilt down to an appreciably smaller amount.

The edible bracken fern shoot, often called "fiddleneck," for obvious reasons, is gathered early in the spring.

Dip the greens out of the pot and fill clean canning jars to within one inch of the top. Then dip up the boiling water, in which they were cooked, filling the jar to within an inch of the top with the water. Add one teaspoon of salt to quarts or ½ teaspoon to pints, if desired.

Wipe the rim of the jar clean and place a hot, previously boiled new lid on the jar and screw down a ring, firmly tight. Place in warm canner. Process the jars (all types of greens) at 10 pounds pressure for 90 minutes (quarts) or 70 minutes (pints). Adjust pounds of pressure, as needed for altitudes above 1,000 feet, if necessary. See your canning book for directions.

Wild greens, canned in this way, will stay wholesome and tasty nearly indefinitely. Be sure to mark the jars, regarding what type of green you have canned. I neglected to do this and can never tell what type of greens I am serving at a meal; we play "guess the green" while we eat. Is it spinach? Pigweed? Lamb's quarters? Oh well, they are all great eating.

While these and more wild greens are great eating, one more of our favorite spring wild food is not really a green, but appears at the same time.

Fiddleneck ferns

In the early spring, the tender shoots of ferns poke up suddenly through pine needles and debris of the forest floor. The shoots of bracken fern and ostrich fern are edible and very good. While the bracken fern is toxic when mature and eaten in bulk, the new shoots are edible and taste like asparagus.

Fiddlenecks (fern shoots that have a small curl at the top, resembling the neck of a violin) are covered with a fuzzy, papery sheath. They must be picked before the leaves appear, or the stem becomes woody and tasteless.

Like asparagus, pick the youngest shoots, just after they emerge, cutting off just below the surface with a sharp knife. Wipe the papery and fuzzy membrane off as well as possible, then simply steam or boil until just tender. Remove from the pot and wipe off any clinging membrane or fuzz. Serve with butter or a cream sauce as you would asparagus and you have truly delectable eating.

Fiddlenecks can be home-canned to enjoy during the winter. In some parts of the country, they are harvested heavily just for this use. Process as you would asparagus after you have cleaned the stalks of their fuzz and membrane.

Some folks regard wild greens as a "survival" food. This is not giving them enough credit. While hundreds of wild foods are edible, these wild greens are truly scrumptious eating, deserving of being added to regular homestead meals. I hope you, like us, never quite regard a "weed" in the same light again. Δ

A self-reliance guide from BACKWOODS HOME Magazine

Clover:

from livestock forage to medicinal tea, this humble plant is one of nature's best gifts

By Eugene Mitchell

Whether young or old, lying in the grass and searching for four-leafed clovers is timeless fun. Sometimes they're so elusive, like the leprechaun, it seems they don't exist. We can find the more common leaves-of-three, though, nearly anyplace we look: in yards, pastures, forest meadows, and of course, there's the Irish Shamrock chosen by St. Patrick as a symbol of the Trinity. Clover is even the state flower of Vermont. We see it growing along roadsides, in the clover-leaf-shaped entrances and exits of interstate highways, and it pops up in music, too:

"I'm looking over a four leaf clover that I overlooked before."

Even if we can't find a four-leaf clover or a leprechaun, we're still lucky. Clover is one of nature's best gifts to life on earth, a boon for humans, animals, plants, even dirt, and through time, wise people have not overlooked this amazing legume, Clover (*Trifolium*).

All legumes, like clover, are able to take free nitrogen from the air to fix in nodules on their roots, called "nitrogen fixing." This is the way legumes, such as clover, provide themselves with the nitrogen they need to grow. The excess is left in the soil in a form that is much easier utilized than chemical fertilizers and in greater quantities than fertilizers or manures. True organic farming and gardening is nearly impossible without legumes in the crop rotation. Since clovers rate as some of the highest nitrogen-fixing plants, second only to alfalfa, clover is excellent for conditioning soil.

Soil conditioner

Used as a winter cover crop, clover replenishes the soil's nitrogen, and its roots bring micro-nutrients closer to the surface. Tilled or plowed under in the spring as a green manure, clover returns phosphorus and potassium to the soil. In warmer regions with longer growing seasons, it's possible to plant clover early in the spring, even a couple of weeks before the last frost, to condition soil for summer planting. With either fall or spring planting, it's excellent in a rotation with heavy nitrogen feeders like corn or tomatoes. If the variety of clover grown is large and the growth thick, it may be necessary to cut the clover before turning it under.

Clover leaves help prevent erosion during heavy rains by catching the raindrops, slowing them, and keeping them from pelting the dirt. The rain drips from the leaves or drains down the stalks, giving the soil time to absorb the water.

Most of us are familiar with white Dutch clover (*T. repens*) that grows so readily in yards with its recognizable three leaves. We also have, in addition to white clover, red (*T. pratense*), crimson (*T. incarnatum*), hop (*T. aureum*), Alsike (*T. hybridum*), Ladino (*T. repens* forma *lodigense*), and many other varieties. Some people wonder if crimson and red clover are the same, but they're not. If their names don't cause enough confusion, they also look alike and can easily be mistaken as

A self-reliance guide from Backwoods Home Magazine

A groundhog eating red clover. Groundhogs, or gophers, are just one of many wild animals that eat clover.

the same plant. Once you see their differences, though, it's easy to identify them, even when they're not side-by-side.

Under good conditions, they both grow to similar heights, the red a little taller. Red's green leaflets have a lighter green "V" in the middle, like a chevron. The flower is light red, a magenta hue, sometimes tending to a light purple. Crimson's green leaflets are notched, and the flower is elongated, conical shaped, and is a dark red color.

Individual varieties of clover are adapted to the various climates and soil conditions in different regions of the country. Red clover likes plenty of water but not extremes of temperature. Alsike clover is adapted for soil with poor drainage and fertility and will thrive in cool climates. Alsike is used mostly as a hay crop and is more nutritious than red clover, but yields less hay. In the Northeast, Ladino, a giant version of white clover, is used as forage and is appreciated because of its robust nitrogen fixing and its "creep." Ladino is regularly grown in the Southeast, too.

Forage for livestock

Optimally, livestock forage should provide the nutrients stock need without additional feed, and for that, legumes are the best. Clovers, along with alfalfa and other legumes, provide protein, fiber, calcium, vitamins A and D, more per acre than any other forage. In the southeastern United States, where I live, clovers thrive in spring, then die off in the hot summer. The grasses sown in pasture mixes, such as fescue and orchard grass, take over until the cooler fall when the clovers begin to grow back.

It's best to graze clover when the leaves are young, before it makes a flower. It's most nutritious then. It's also best as a green manure during this pre-flower stage.

Ladino is grown across the U.S. and Canada, and it makes a large amount of forage with its considerable size. It can last a long time, if managed well, and because of its creep, it's possible to sow an acre with just a pound or two of seeds. For a thicker crop during its first growing season, you can plant up to six pounds per acre.

Care must be taken when grazing cattle on clover alone. If stock come from a poorer pasture directly onto a rich clover field, there is the risk of bloat, and bloat can be fatal to cattle.

For questions about your specific area, ask the folks at your local feed store or your local agricultural extension agent.

Grouse, partridge, and quail eat the foliage of clover, depending on what area of the U.S. you're in. Small mammals, such as groundhogs, cottontails, marmots, and others, also eat clover. I live on an old farmstead in northeast Georgia with clovers in the pasture mix, and I regularly see whitetails and groundhogs browsing the edges of the field, as well as wild turkeys and rabbits. Seed companies, like Pennington, offer seed mixes to plant as food plots for wildlife, some of which contain clovers as an integral part of the mix. Some mixes, notably those for whitetail deer, are completely clovers. You can find products such as these at a feed or farm supply store.

Honey

Clover is a strong attraction for honeybees, also. Clover, as a single source, accounts for more honey than any other source in the United States. It is a light, amber honey that sweetens without overwhelming. In the U.S., sweet and white clover account for the most honey produced.

For humans, commercially grown clover sprouts are available in supermarkets and health food stores. They fill salad bowls with delicious crunch and taste, and they're good just by themselves as a snack. They contain a variety of nutrients, such as magnesium, calcium, potassium, chromium, vitamin C, thiamin, and niacin, and are naturally low in carbohydrates. When sprouting clover or any other seed for the table, use only true organic, untreated, seeds.

Traditional sources tell us that while mature clover leaves are edible, they can cause bloat in humans, too, unless soaked for several hours in salt water or boiled for 10 minutes or so.

Through time, clover has been used for a variety of medicinal purposes. Native Americans used white clover leaf tea for colds and fevers, and Europeans, who introduced clover to America, used clover flower tea for arthritis and gout. Traditionally, red clover flower tea has been recommended for breast cancer, prostate cancer, as a blood purifier, an anti-coagulant, a mild sedative, a spasmodic, for asthma, and as an externally applied treatment for skin sores and cancers. It is an alterative, which means that it changes the conditions of the tissues, increasing blood flow and cleansing the blood. It is suggested as a spring tonic for those blood purifying and detoxifying qualities.

Red clover is being examined by today's medical science as possible treatment for pre- and post-menopausal symptoms. Researchers have found that red clover contains isoflavones, or phytoestrogens. Phytoestrogens are plant-based compounds that exhibit modest estrogenic and anti-estrogen qualities, depending on pre-existing estrogen levels. Tests are inconclusive and sometimes contradictory, but experimentation continues.

Clover is abundant in the wild or easily grown by anyone. It gives benefits to the entire strata of life on earth. We are all, everyone and everything, lucky to have such a humble and generous charm as clover.

Health

Red clover is commercially available dried, in capsules, tablets, and tinctures. Two commercially available products specifically for women are Promensil and Rimostil.

As with harvesting any wild food, when cutting red clover flowers for tea, use common sense, and cut those flowers you know to be clean of contaminants not those by a roadway, or near a trash can, or that have been sprayed with any chemicals, and don't cut those in pastures with grazing stock. Gently rinse them. I wrap them in cheesecloth and hang them in a shady place out of the rain, where the wind circulates.

Soil conditioning

Any clover *Trifolium* is a good soil conditioner, but some are better than others. Properly managed clovers with the highest nitrogen fixing abilities per acre, highest to lowest, are: Ladino, Alsike, Sweet, Red, White.

All fix over 100 pounds, with Ladino fixing 170 pounds or more. Crimson will fix between 90 and 100 pounds. White clover in a mowed yard is always small, of course, but it can grow over a foot in a field, while the others in the list can grow two feet or more.

A partial list of widely grown clovers and poundage to sow per acre: Ladino 1-6; Crimson 20-25; Red 10-15; White 6-8.

Clover can be sown, generally, in the fall a month or so before the first frost, or after the last frost in spring. In regions with mild winters, it can be sown a few weeks before the last frost in spring to get an early start on soil conditioning for summer rotation. If you have a big plot, you might want to use a seed spreader. If not, just broadcast by hand. After sowing, cover the seeds with about ½" of soil and pack the soil lightly. Planting before a rain shower is a good idea, but if a rain shower isn't wandering by, a good watering by hand will help. Dampen the soil enough to wet it, but not enough to make it muddy.

Depending on the weather, they dry in a few weeks. You can dry them inside on a flat sheet, in a commercially available dryer, or an oven, but I prefer to let the air dry them.

After they have dried, store them in an airtight glass jar or plastic bag. After a few days, if there is moisture showing at the top of the jar or bag, they're not dry enough. Take them out and dry them a bit longer. My experience is that red clover flowers don't crumble when dry, but will fall apart if you rub them between your fingers. Also, they'll feel a little soft, but not brittle.

Clover tea is brewed just like any other tea. Don't boil the dried flowers; instead pour boiling water over a heaping tablespoon or two of flowers, and let them steep for about 10 minutes. Drink the tea hot or iced, and of course, you can sweeten it with a dollop of clover honey. For health, the recommended dosage is three cups a day.

Clover leaf tea is light with a delicate taste, and not astringent. Δ

Stinging Nettle:
Mother Nature's healthiest pick

By Linda Gabris

Mother nature has many wonderful plants for foraging but if I had to pick a favorite, I think I'd point a gloved finger at stinging nettle. It is a number one pick for good health and fine eating.

My grandmother, an herbalist in the rural woods where I grew up, always said that nothing enlivened the spirit or rejuvenated the body better or faster than a cup of stinging nettle tea commonly known as "spring" tonic—for it'll put bounce in your step. "Half the cure," she'd wink, "is in the drinking. The other half comes from time spent gathering…"

Nettles belong to the Urtica family with more than 500 world species—the majority being tropical members. Common stinging nettles occur in more temperate climates across North America. Since nettles are plentiful and easy to identify, they are an ideal pick for beginner foragers and can be enjoyed from early spring to the last days of summer.

Like dandelions, nettles are considered a nasty weed by gardeners and land owners. The hearty plant can thrive anywhere and once root has taken, it has a tendency to spread like crazy. Nettles can be found filling waste grounds, but for kitchen use you'll want to harvest from a woodland patch where the nettles will be cleaner and more lush than those found forcing their way up through rotting boards, cracked cement, and broken pavement. You'll find nettles growing in abundance on moist grounds around swamps, marshes, along waterways, and in open areas of woodlands. In fact, there will be a nettle patch thriving wherever the wind has carried seed.

Mature average-sized nettles measure two to four feet high but on fertile grounds they can reach over six feet tall. They have square, fibrous stems and long, sharp, finely-toothed leaves that are covered with tiny hollow hairs filled with compounds including histamine, acetylcholine, and formic acid, which causes a stinging sensation when touched—thus its name. This is the number one key to identification and you will only want to make the test once.

Mature stinging nettle with flowers

You'll need long pants tucked inside socks, long-sleeved shirt, and gloves for harvesting. Don't fret if you do get stung, as the burning sensation and rash, if one develops, only causes discomfort in most folks for about an hour and does not permanently harm skin. You should leave your dog at home on this outing, especially if he's short-haired, as contact might be unpleasant.

An oddity of nature is that the best antidote for nettle sting is the juice of its own leaves, but if you're not armed for picking you're bound to get stung again going in for the cure. In this case, it's better to hunt down some burdock leaves, moss, or damp birch bark which will help relieve accidental sting. Some outdoor enthusiasts carry a baggie of baking soda which can be mixed with water into paste for emergency relief. The leaves lose the sting upon drying and cooking.

Nettles have greenish clusters of "beady" flowers that appear in midsummer dangling from the junction of the leaf stem. The flower develops into seeds that spread by wind and take root easily. Since the plant also spreads by root, it's easy to see why they are so plentiful.

As far back as history dates, stinging nettles have been praised as a "cure-all." Modern research is looking at nettle preparations as treatment for various conditions including prostate cancer and hepatitis. Studies have shown the herb useful in treating urinary disorders.

Since nettles are rich in calcium, magnesium, iron, potassium, phosphorous, silica, iodine, sodium, sulfur, and other elements including tannin, beta-carotene, and amino acids, it is easy to understand why the herb is highly regarded in the world of herbal medicine. Nettles are also a good source of vitamins C and B complex and they are said to dish up more protein than any other vegetable.

North American aboriginal medicine men and herbalists have used nettles as treatment for gout, goiter, anemia, thin blood, epilepsy, poor circulation, pinworms, depression, intestinal disorder, diarrhea, and for flushing impurities from the kidneys and bladder. Probably the most shocking account of nettle use is an old English claim that paralyzed limbs could be brought back to life by flogging with a whip of nettles. From this, no doubt, stemmed the belief that the plant directly applied could ease pain of rheumatism, arthritis, and swollen joints.

Nettle infusions and powdered plant are noted for having power to stop hemorrhaging, internal bleeding, and excessive flow from wounds and cuts. When I was a kid I was prone to nosebleed and Grandma always had a bottle of nettle juice handy for when I was struck. A ball of cloth dabbed in juice, then inserted in my nose stopped the flow promptly. The potion was also applied to cuts, scratches, and bug bites as disinfectant and healer.

I still depend on Grandma's treatment for cold and flu—nettle tea sweetened with honey and heavy on lemon—to break up congestion. Bronchitis, asthma, and pneumonia have been treated with nettle concoctions for ages with one remedy calling for the sufferer to inhale smoke of dried burnt nettle leaves. Recent studies indicate that nettles, as a natural antihistamine, provide relief for allergies like hay fever without harmful side effects often associated with pharmaceutical antihistamines. As any seasonal sufferer knows, this discovery is certainly nothing to sneeze at. On the lighter side of good health and well-being, nettles can help grow thicker hair, clearer skin, and stronger nails.

During World War I, the fibrous stems were used in Germany like flax to replace the shortage of cotton to make army clothing and bandages. During times of need, nettles were also cut down and dried and used as animal fodder which is reported as being both nutritious and well-received. Domestic ducks and geese are said to have better tasting fat after gorging on nettles, and Grandma mixed chopped dried nettles into chicken feed, swearing it increased egg production. My dad kept a ready scythe to chop down nettles that grew around the horse stables. Once hung and dried, the leaves were stripped and added to feed rations to give the team shiny coats and, according to dad, the supplement was good for the horses' digestive systems.

Nettles can be harvested from the earliest shoots of spring at which time they are most potent for medicinal uses. The leaves can be harvested all summer long for use as fresh tea, for drying, or as table greens. Once the leaves take on the crisp of autumn they begin to toughen and lose much of their nutritional value.

Here are some of my favorite uses for nettles. It's a wonderful way to cash in on the healthy rewards of springtime.

Stinging nettle hair tonic. When I was little, Grandma used this nettle rinse on my hair after washing and I must admit, my braids could take a good tugging. The solution can be used as a comb-through for thinning hair or as a deterrent for balding. To make hair tonic, simmer four quarts of fresh picked nettle leaves in one quart of water for three hours or until infusion is strong. Cover and let steep until cold. Strain. Add ½ cup cider vinegar. Bottle and cork. This can be massaged into scalp as a dandruff treatment.

"Spring" tonic—fresh nettle tea. Good to the last drop and rich in minerals and vitamins to boot. Put a handful of fresh washed leaves into a heated tea pot. Cover with boiling water and steep for five minutes, or until desired strength is reached. Strain before serving. Especially nice with a dab of honey. Refrigerate leftover tea for a healthy cold drink. Cold tea also makes nutritious houseplant water and leaves or dregs can be sprinkled on soil for a boost.

To dry nettles

If you want to stash some sunshine away for winter use, there's no better way than filling up the baskets with nettle leaves for drying. Dried leaves can be steeped into delicious tea that makes an invigorating morning drink and since it's caffeine-free, it can be enjoyed by the younger set as well. Use two teaspoons of dried nettles per pint of boiling water for table or afternoon tea and increase to three to four teaspoons per pint for medicinal tea. To dry young nettles, pick leaves and spread on paper or screens and let dry in an airy place until crispy. Larger, more mature plants—even those in flower—can be cut down at lower stalk, tied into bundles, and hung in an airy place until dry, about five to seven days. When crisp, strip off leaves and dried flowers and crush. Store in tea tins.

Nettle sprinkle. Crushed dried nettles can be used in place of dried parsley for adding enlivening color to any dish calling for a sprinkle of greenery. Use it to dress up cottage cheese, eggs, dumplings, or anything in need of zap. Use hands to crush leaves to same consistency as parsley.

Nettle salt substitute. In later parts of summer when nettle flowers go to seed, they can be gathered, dried, pulverized, and used as a salt substitute. Simply spread the seedy clusters on paper towels or screens and dry in an airy place about a week. Pulverize with mortar and pestle or in a blender. Fill shaker and use in place of salt. If you find it's not salty enough, add a teaspoon of salt per shaker. You'll still be cutting down your intake by a good percentage. This was originally used as a goiter treatment because of its iodine content.

Stinging nettle potherb. Cooked nettles are similar in taste to spinach, only I find they are milder and more tender, especially when young. They can be used in place of spinach or Swiss Chard in any recipe calling for cooked greens. Boil until tender in salted water and drain, or steam leaves until tender. Dress as you would any potherb with a dab of butter, sprinkle of cheese, cream sauce, spray of lemon juice, shake of herbs, or use in quiche or pudding.

Aunt Nettie's nettle quiche. This recipe was handed down to me from my grandma who got it from her Aunt Nettie. It makes a delicious pie to serve for Sunday brunch or as a light supper to enjoy after a day spent in the field picking nettles.

10-inch unbaked pie shell
1 cup grated sharp cheddar cheese
2 cups cooked nettles, drained
¼ cup minced onion
4 eggs
¾ cup light cream or milk
salt, pepper, cayenne to taste

Sprinkle cheese in bottom of chilled pie shell. Spread prepared nettles over cheese. Beat remaining ingredients and pour over nettles. Bake in 400° F oven for 10 minutes. Reduce heat to 350° F and bake another 20 minutes or until custard is set and knife inserted comes out clean.

Delicious cream of nettle soup. This is my all-time favorite soup and it can be made throughout the growing season from April onward.

```
1 pound nettle leaves
2 Tbsp. oil or butter
1 minced onion
4 tsp. chopped chives
3 Tbsp. flour
2 cups hot chicken stock
1 cup water
2 tsp. seasoned salt
1 tsp. fresh ground pepper
1 cup cream
nutmeg, if desired
```

Heat oil or melt butter in soup pot. Sauté onion until soft. Add chives and flour and stir until blended. Slowly stir in stock, beating with a wooden spoon until smooth. Add remaining ingredients, except cream, and heat to boiling. Reduce heat and simmer 20 minutes. Add cream and heat to just boiling. Taste and adjust seasoning, if needed. Rub soup through a sieve into heated tureen. Sprinkle with nutmeg, if desired.

Old world stinging nettle wilt. Wilts are Old World salads that call for greens to be steeped in boiling spiced vinegar then cooled, drained, and served as a side dish to accompany roast meat or fish.

```
1 colander washed nettle tops
1 thinly sliced onion, red is especially nice
½ green or red pepper, thinly sliced
1 cup vinegar (white, malt, apple, or spiced)
½ cup water
1 tsp. salt
1 tsp. mustard seed
3 tsp. sugar
```

Bring all ingredients except nettles, onion, and peppers to boil in kettle. Reduce heat and simmer 10 minutes. Add nettle leaves and cook 2 minutes. Remove from heat. Put onion and pepper in heat-proof bowl and pour hot nettle mixture on top. Cover and let steep until cold. Drain and serve in small individual bowls.

Grandma's nettle wine. Every season I make a gallon or two of nettle wine from Grandma's old recipe. This fine white wine is a prize in any cellar. Sip it mulled for cold and flu treatment. A little glass before bedtime helps induce sleep.

> 8 quarts washed nettle leaves
> 2 gallons water
> 3 thinly sliced, unpeeled lemons
> 1 ginger root, grated
> 12 cups sugar
> 1 slice stale toast
> 1 package yeast

Put nettles in large kettle. Add ½ gallon of water and bring to a boil. Add lemon and ginger. Reduce heat and simmer for 1 hour. Put sugar in wine making vat, strain liquid onto sugar, and stir until dissolved. Add remaining water and stir. Cover with cloth and allow to cool. When cool, sprinkle yeast on toast and float on liquid. Cover and let stand in warm room for five days. Pour into fermentation jar, put on air-lock and let work until bubbling ceases. Siphon into sterilized bottles and cork. Δ

Harvesting the wild: Asparagus

By Jackie Clay

Picking wild asparagus is often the first step a person takes toward learning to forage wild food. Although not technically a "wild" plant, more of an escapee from gardens via seeds and birds, asparagus grows very wild in most places across the US and Canada. And, because fresh dew-covered wild asparagus is completely delectable, both raw and lightly cooked, it is well worth the hunt.

Finding wild asparagus

Wild asparagus is one plant that is easier to locate during the winter and early spring than it is mid-spring. Therefore, the best scouting for your asparagus is during these months. You'll be looking for "bushes" of asparagus fern, often dotted with red "berries"—the seeds of the female plants. In the summer and fall, these asparagus bushes are bright green. Mature, heavily-rooted asparagus bushes can grow waist high or higher, and are bigger around than a person can hug. They are light and airy, with delicate leaves.

In the winter, the plants turn a bright yellow, which fades to a yellowish tan with time. The color makes the bushes stand out among snow and stark grass and bare branches.

Most wild asparagus is found along roadsides, usually along fences or irrigation ditches (in the west). After all, seed is eaten by birds and birds perch on fences. We know what those birds do, besides perch, right? Instant fertilized asparagus seeds. Likewise, you'll also often find asparagus growing on the south sides of trees and along brushy edges of farm fields. Those good old birds, again.

Irrigation ditches both distribute fallen seed and water the plants as they germinate and grow to maturity.

Another good bet is around abandoned old homestead and farm sites. Often old garden asparagus has spread to quite large patches by means of dropped seeds and those birds again. Of course, always get permission to explore and pick asparagus on private property. The roadside is public domain in most areas.

David Clay loves picking asparagus.

Drive around quiet country lanes and roadsides slowly, watching for asparagus bushes. Take a notebook and a map of the area. Also, bring a skein of red yarn. Your first asparagus plant may be a bit hard to discover, but once you see what you're looking for they're easy to spot. If in doubt, take an experienced gardener along on your first exploration trip. I also know of no poisonous plant that can be confused with asparagus.

Stop! There's a couple of plants over there by that old fence. Park your vehicle safely and take out your map, marking an "X" where you found your asparagus. Now take a piece of yarn a foot long or so and tie a nice bow in a conspicuous place near, but not on, the plant. If there are several plants nearby in the general vicinity, make note in your notebook, but don't tie more bows. You don't want to alert other asparagus hunters. And there are a lot of folks who hunt asparagus in the spring.

Continue your exploration, making notes in your notebook, marking Xs on your map, and tying red yarn bows to help remind you where those plants are. Remember, during mid-spring when you'll return to pick your tender spears, the weeds, grass, and brush will be lush and will partially hide your quarry.

Should you not begin to hunt asparagus until the spring, simply watch for green, mature asparagus plants. Then stop and cut the entire plant off below the surface of the ground and mark your location by yarn and in your notebook. I toss the plant off, as other hunters would be happy to cut your patch. No need in making it too easy by leaving the cut plant.

Cautions about picking wild asparagus

Be careful *not* to pick wild asparagus where there is a possibility of agricultural chemicals or county road weed killers having been sprayed on your future food. I don't pick asparagus close to heavily cropped areas, especially orchards (with plenty of spraying). Hayfields, pastures, and woods are generally safe neighbors to your wild asparagus bed.

I also stay clear of asparagus growing next to very busy highways or an expressway because of heavy fumes from traffic. While gasoline sold today is lead-free, lead stays in the soil for a long, long time, and I'd just as soon eat lead-free wild asparagus.

Picking asparagus

Asparagus begins to grow in early mid-spring. This time differs, depending on the growing zone and weather you live in. It's generally about right to begin hunting asparagus spears when the spring grass is beginning to grow well. You won't find asparagus coming up before the grass is growing, but if you wait too long, it'll be harder to find because the rank grass will hide it until it is over-mature.

I carry a large basket and a small, sharp pocketknife. You want the most tender asparagus you can find. So don't pick in the heat of the day. I go out, first thing in the morning, often when the dew is still heavy on the grass. The asparagus spears you harvest then will be melt-in-your-mouth tender.

The ideal spear will be fat, the tip tightly closed and perhaps eight inches tall. The top will be purplish green and the lower portion will be white. These spears grow quickly—overnight, it seems. Unfortunately, the taller they grow, the tougher and more woody the spear gets. Taste store-bought asparagus to see what I mean. But even the longer spears can be harvested. Just cut the whole thing off at or below ground level, then snap the top off with your fingers where it will break. Throw the lower part away, and keep the top; you have the most tender part of the long spear.

You can either cut the spears with a sharp knife, at or below ground level, or snap them off with your thumb and first finger, right at ground level.

Notice that we cut all asparagus off at ground level, even the tough, longer spears. This is to keep the plant producing. Some folks mistakenly let the long spears go and just harvest the tender spears poking up nearby. Unfortunately this signals the plant to quit producing spears and production abruptly stops, leaving only the one tall fern to mature.

For this reason, you need to cut off all mature ferns from any plant group you want to harvest. If you come on a mature patch, simply cut all ferns off, toss 'em away, and return in about a week. You'll find a nice bunch of tender spears poking out of the grass, just waiting for you.

If I'm seriously hunting wild asparagus to can or dehydrate for the pantry, along with a good batch to eat, of course, I take a cooler with a layer of ice on the bottom. Over the ice goes a folded bath towel to keep the asparagus off the ice, yet cool. In a good day of hunting, we can fill a large cooler.

I always "pay off" informants with a nice batch of my best asparagus. Some folks are too old to hunt asparagus any more, but can point out a great patch. Others hunt it on occasion, but really don't want to bother. We greatly appreciate such tips and are generous with thanks and tender asparagus spears as well.

The best thing about asparagus (other than the taste) is that it is a cut-and-come-again plant. During the growing season, which extends over about a month, you can cut a batch and return in about four days to find as many or more spears rising up out of the grass to greet you.

Taming the wild asparagus

Not all wild plants take to being tamed, nor would you especially want them in your garden. We harvest bunches of lambs quarter and pig weed every year, but I certainly wouldn't advise anyone to plant them in their garden.

But asparagus is happy to be domesticated. Of course there are more productive varieties of hybrid asparagus, such as the nearly all-male Jersey King and Jersey Knight. They put all their energy into producing spears, instead of seeds, and the spears are large and fat. But sometimes cash is tight or you might actually want seeds to enlarge your asparagus plot. So consider the not-so-lowly wild asparagus.

I try to dig wild asparagus roots in the early spring, about the time the first shoots are being sent up. In this way, the plant has a good chance to recover from being divided and transplanted before winter comes.

One large, vigorous asparagus clump can provide you with a couple of dozen plants. The clump is formed of many individual plants, some quite large-rooted, some small. And they are all tangled with each other, making dividing them quite an interesting project.

Take a sharp spade and dig the entire clump up. First dig out away from the obvious spears, in a circle about eighteen inches in diameter, down about two feet. Then, carefully pry under the plant, from all sides, working it loose. You will sweat and dig for half an hour if you dig carefully, so as not to injure the roots. Take sod and all. You'll end up with what appears to be a dehydrated octopus with many, many fat, long roots. At this point, I carefully work loose one entire plant and replant it in the hole and tenderly cover it up. I never take all of anything, leaving something to reproduce, to go to seed, or to feed others.

If there is a body of water nearby, carry/drag the clump to the water and soak it well, working away grass roots and soil. When you finish, there will be just the tangled asparagus plants. Now sit down in the shade and gently work the plants apart. Each has a crown, possibly with a tiny spear shoot budded at its top. And each has several long, brown fattish roots dangling down, from six inches to two feet.

As you free a plant, lay it under a damp burlap sack, in the shade. When you finish, you will often have more than a dozen nice, healthy plants—and no grass roots—to take home to your garden. Of course, you can repeat this process at different locations until you have as many free plants as you need. Remember, though, don't dig plants from someone else's land without permission. You sure wouldn't want someone digging plants up on your land.

As asparagus likes to be well fed, your new home for the wildlings should be well tilled, with a good bucket of rotted compost worked in where each plant will be set out. Dig a trench six inches deeper than the plant, allowing the roots to be spread out, but not bent and doubled up. Make a mound in the center and gently spread the roots out down its sides. Fill in the trench to the point that the crown is covered a bit. Then water well. Continue until all are happily planted.

As the spears grow, gradually fill in the trench until it is level with the soil around it. Then add a straw mulch over the row to hold back the weeds. Your wild asparagus is still spirited, but contentedly domesticated. And it will grow on, nearly forever, with very little special attention.

Home canning wild asparagus

Wild asparagus is very easy to home can. First, rinse and sort your asparagus. I choose the fattest, most tender spears to can as full spears, and the rest I cut into pieces.

Because asparagus is a low-acid food, as are all vegetables, it must be canned with a pressure canner. I recommend canning your asparagus the same day you pick it, as it doesn't take too long before it gets tough or limp, just like store asparagus. Simply put a big tea kettle of fresh water on, along with a pan to boil your jar lids in. Then, while the water is boiling, cut the spears into your jars. I cut off the tough lower end. With a sharp knife begin cutting off first the very bottom, then on up an inch at a time, until your knife easily cuts the spear. The tougher ends may be simmered and put through a sieve for asparagus soup, canned at the same time you do your spears and/or pieces of asparagus.

I can both spears and inch-long pieces of asparagus. I can the spears in wide mouth jars, the pieces in regular jars, as the price of regular lids is much lower. But it's much easier to get full spears neatly out of a wide mouth jar.

Pack the jars snugly to within an inch of the top of the jar. Then add half a teaspoonful of salt to pints and fill the jars to within an inch of the top with boiling water.

Wipe the rim of the jar clean, place a hot, previously boiled lid on, and screw the ring down firmly tight. Place the jars in a warm canner and process the jars at 10 pounds pressure (unless you live at an altitude above 1,000 feet; check

> **The health benefits of asparagus**
>
> Since ancient times asparagus has been thought to have special health properties.
>
> Today we know it is not only a good source of folic acid and vitamin C, it also contains goodly amounts of disease-fighting antioxidant carotenoids that your body also uses to make vitamin A.
>
> According to the National Cancer Institute, of all foods tested, asparagus contains the greatest amount of *glutathione*, one of the body's most potent cancer fighters.
>
> It is also high in *rutin*, which is valuable for strengthening the blood vessels.

canning manual for directions) for 30 minutes (pints) or 40 minutes (quarts).

Dehydrating asparagus

It is easy to successfully dehydrate asparagus at home. I dry quite a bit as it is so handy to use in mixed vegetables and soups.

I pick out the nicest spears I have and rinse them well. Cut them into one-inch pieces and blanch for about three minutes; do not overdo the cooking.

Place in a single layer on your dehydrator trays and dehydrate at 125 degrees until brittle. If my spears are very fat, over half an inch thick, I also cut the pieces in half so they dry quickly. This also makes them rehydrate much faster.

Store the dried asparagus in airtight containers in a cool, dark place. My bottom cupboard shelves hold my dehydrated foods successfully, and the jars are handy, too.

To rehydrate the asparagus, simmer until tender in twice as much water as asparagus. Or add the dry asparagus to your soup or stew a half an hour before serving.

Recipes for using all that delectable asparagus

One of our favorite recipes for wild asparagus is to carry a jar of ranch dressing with us, right into the fields, holding it on the ice with the asparagus. Then, as we finish, we sit down in the shade with a loaf of homemade French bread, butter, and cheese and dip the raw asparagus in the ranch dressing. It doesn't get much better than that.

Another very easy and simple way to fix wild asparagus is to steam it in very little water until just nicely tender and serve hot with an herbed or lemon butter. This is the way I serve the whole asparagus spears and I don't get many complaints.

An old family favorite is creamed asparagus over hearty homemade toast. I like the toast to be either a good sourdough or honey whole wheat. Home baked, of course.

Simply simmer or steam the asparagus until tender; you can use fresh or dehydrated. (Or use a jar of your home canned asparagus.) Don't cook it too long or you'll have mush, not wonderful asparagus.

In a medium saucepan, add two tablespoons of butter, melted, and two tablespoons of white flour. Stir well. Then add either a cup and a half of low fat milk or cream, whichever your arteries will stand. Of course, cream is best, but not many of us can dare eat as we wish. Add a pinch of salt and black pepper to taste. Simmer while stirring to make a medium-thick white sauce. Add more milk, if necessary. Then drain and gently blend in cooked asparagus. Set aside in a warm place.

Slice your bread and toast it. Lay out on a plate. Spoon on creamed asparagus and enjoy.

Another of our favorites is asparagus au gratin. This is a cheesie baked dish, quick to put together, and always appreciated on the table.

Asparagus au gratin

---
2 lbs. tender wild asparagus spears
1 cup sharp cheddar cheese, grated
2 Tbsp. butter
2 Tbsp. flour
1 tsp. salt
pinch black pepper
1 cup buttered cracker or dry bread bits
1 cup milk or cream

Butter a baking dish, put in whole asparagus spears or cut pieces in layers, sprinkling grated cheese between the layers.

In a small saucepan, melt the butter and stir in the flour. Cook a minute. Add the milk (or cream), salt, and pepper. Stir well until thickened to a medium white sauce. Pour this over asparagus. Cover with crumbs and grated cheese. Bake at 300° F until nicely browned.

Asparagus can also be used in salads, either as one ingredient in a mixed salad, raw, or lightly steamed and chilled and used in any of several salads. My personal favorite is:

Two beans and wild asparagus salad

½ cup cut wax beans
½ cup canned red kidney beans or other red bean
½ cup cut asparagus spears
4 Tbsp. vegetable oil
4 Tbsp. vinegar
2 Tbsp. sugar or honey

Cook the vegetables until tender. Drain well. Make your dressing by mixing the oil, vinegar, and sugar. You may also add a bit of French dressing if you wish. Toss the vegetables with the dressing and place, covered, in refrigerator to marinate well. Serve chilled.

Wild asparagus can be used any way you use peas in shepherd's pie, stews, soups, salads, pot pies, pasties, casseroles, or our favorite of favorites, raw, right from the wild patch. Seasoned with nothing but fresh, cold dew drops, this wild foraged vegetable can't be beat. Δ

Harvesting the wild: Flower buds

By Jackie Clay

When you've had a long day out in the fields, you deserve a break. And a bud. No, I don't mean a beer. I mean a good meal, featuring, of all things, flower buds. Now before you toss this down, think about it. You are probably very familiar with several flower buds, commonly eaten in most homes: broccoli, cauliflower, and artichokes. I don't know how many times I've gotten busy with other things, only to go out in the garden to pick one of these, and find that I was too late. The buds were in full flower, past their prime as a vegetable.

In the wild, there are many, many flowers and flower buds that are not only *edible*, but actually choice fare for the table. Native Americans regularly dined on these tender, seasonal delights. If you've been following the *Harvesting the Wild* series, you've already learned about dandelion and cholla buds. Let's take a look at several other common buds and tasty flowers available to us. While they are most often thought of as "survival" foods, they form an extended garden for our family, and many other backwoods dwellers.

A self-reliance guide from Backwoods Home Magazine

Milkweed

Nearly everyone is familiar with the common milkweed, with its large oval leaves and seed pods that pop open in the fall, sending fluffy parachutes sailing through the air. As these dry seed pods remain on the dead plant through the winter, it's usually easy to identify the next spring's milkweed patch. As with all wild plants, the wild forager should make sure the plant is the common milkweed before consuming any part.

As the milkweed gains mature height, clusters of buds form and begin to open. These flat clusters of buds open to lavender flowers. The best time to harvest milkweed buds is when they are tightly closed. Snip these buds from the plant and gather a nice bowlful. To eat, simply bring a pan of water to a boil, adding a pinch of salt. Then boil for four minutes. Drain and discard the water. Boil briefly in two more changes of water, then drain and enjoy with butter and a squeeze of lemon, if you desire. Milkweed buds are very good. The reason for the three boilings is to remove any trace of bitterness from the milky sap.

Pink or common milkweed provides many tasty foods throughout the season.

Also very good are the very young milkweed pods. These are best eaten when only an inch or an inch and a half long. Simply pluck these immature pods, then boil for four minutes, draining and discarding the water. As with the buds, boil again for a minute, twice, discarding each water. Then boil for about 10 minutes in fresh, salted water until tender. You will think you're eating okra. And like okra, you can also slice and bread the pre-boiled pods and deep fry them. They taste like okra, but are not as "slimy."

Immature milkweed pods are a valuable addition to meat stews and soups.

Yucca

The common yucca is found just about nationwide. It's tough, pointed, strap-like leaves make it look pretty dry and useless. But you should taste the small, tender flower buds that form along the tall flower stalk in the late spring. Pick the buds when they are quite small and tight and you will think you are eating fresh garden peas. They are very succulent and tender.

Simply pick these buds as you would peas, then boil just enough to make them tender, not mushy. I like them either with a pat of butter and sprinkle of salt, or in a light cream sauce.

Another favorite of mine is to harvest the just-opened yucca flowers on a cool morning. Dip them in your favorite vegetable dip and eat raw or take them home for lunch. While they are still very fresh, you can also dip them in deep frying batter (such as tempura), then deep fry briefly until just crisp and golden brown. They are also excellent served with a sweet and sour dip.

Wild daylily

How about the common wild daylily. This large, showy orange flower forms on a tall stem, accompanied by many other buds, as each flower only stays open for a day, hence its name. The plant is a shaggy bunch of drooping, strap-like leaves. In many areas, the wild daylily fills ditches and roadsides for miles. Not only is the daylily gorgeous, but tasty, as well.

Yes, you can eat the domestic daylily, but with so many new colors and variations it seems almost a shame to eat the flower buds. But if you get tempted, just remember that the flower would only last a single day anyway, and there will be many more very soon.

Daylily buds are best harvested when fairly long, but before they show any sign of opening. I like them dipped in batter and fried, but my very favorite is to make egg foo yung with them. Simply whip up the whites of two eggs per person, add a pinch of salt, and a sprinkle of hot chile, if you like. Then chop several daylily buds, along with one small onion.

Gently fold in beaten egg yolks and vegetables. Fry four-inch wide patties in vegetable oil until done. Serve warm, topped with sweet and sour sauce or traditional egg foo yung sauce, which is 1½ cups chicken broth blended into 1½ Tbsp. cornstarch in a small pan. Stir in 1 tsp. soy sauce, ½ tsp. salt, a dash of black pepper, and a ½ tsp. sugar. Cook over medium heat, stirring constantly. When thickened, serve hot over egg patties. These are very good, and nearly everyone loves them. (Just don't tell folks they're dining on flower foo yung.)

And if these aren't good enough, you must try batter-fried whole, open daylily flowers. I especially like the new hybrid domestic daylilies that have a thicker, ruffled petal. They have more substance than their wild cousins, but the wild daylilies are pretty darned good, as well.

Violet

There are many violet species which grow throughout North America, ranging from white, yellow, and, of course, violet including bi-colored flowers. All are edible. While the leaves can be eaten as one would spinach, as a child my very favorite was violet flowers. The new flowers are crunchy and slightly sweet. You can toss a handful on top of a salad to beautify it. Or throw some in a light-colored Jello dessert after it has cooled a bit. Pioneer children thrilled to violet candy, which was simply moist violets dipped in precious white sugar, then allowed to dry. This creates a delicate shell around the sparkling flower. A very pretty "candy."

Wild violets make an interesting addition to a wild spring salad.

Pumpkin and squash blossoms

While not "wild" in the true sense, you will think the pumpkin and squash vines have run wild by the time they bloom. If you pick the male flowers (the ones that do not have a slight bulb at the base), you will not damage your future crop at all. These flowers are excellent when slightly stir fried with mild chiles and onions. Or you can dip them in tempura batter and deep fry them until golden brown. Serve with your favorite dip. I like them with a bowl of chili and sour cream. Dip them first in the chili, then just a bit of sour cream. They are *so good*.

You can also stuff pumpkin and squash blossoms that are open nearly all the way. Simply mix up your favorite meatloaf recipe, including bread crumbs, then gently stuff each blossom. Tuck the ends of the petals in and repeat until the baking dish is full. Bake at 350° F until almost done, then sprinkle with grated cheese and drizzle catsup over the top. Bake until done. Be ready for raves.

Why don't you try some of these delectable buds and flowers this year? They are so easy and fun to pick, and even easier to prepare and serve. Have a bud....on me. Δ

A self-reliance guide from Backwoods Home Magazine

Wild raspberries: Summertime's finest treat

By Linda Gabris

"One for me," Grandpa would laugh as he smacked his lips loudly, savoring one tangy, juicy raspberry after another. His eyes twinkled as he danced about, making sure that he was safely out of Grandmother's sight. "And," he'd continue, his knobby fingers expertly working amongst the prickly thorns, "one for my pail..." He'd gently place a berry in the large, shiny tin can that dangled from his waist, looped to his belt by its shoestring handle. This left both hands free for picking and eating. Grandmother and I would be rigged up in similar fashion, pails hanging from cloth belts strung around our middles. Only we would actually be busying ourselves trying to fill our pails, whereas Grandpa never collected near as many raspberries as he ate!

Every-so-often on our berry-picking-outings, Grandmother would catch Grandpa pickin' and eatin' and she'd give him a scolding. "No raspberry dumplings for you tonight..." she'd threaten, but Grandpa just couldn't help himself. The berries were too irresistible. Even Grandmother and I would stoop to temptation and sample a few berries while hidden 'neath the fragrant greenery of the woody canes. At the end of the day, berry-stained lips and tongues easily tattled on us all.

"Two for me..." He would hum secretly. "One for my pail. Three for me...One for my pail..."

Regardless of Grandpa's hand to mouth habit, an afternoon of raspberry picking out back of the old sheds, outbuildings, and open wooded areas around our farm would yield a plentiful mess of fragrant, delicious berries. Picking often throughout their growing season—from early July to late August, we'd collect enough berries for Grandmother to make into all our favorite dishes. Besides plenty of berries to use in fresh raspberry pies, tarts, and squares, we also collected enough to do up into treats to last over the winter months, too.

Wild raspberries

Raspberry preserves, syrup, and jam brought colorful summer flavor to our table all year round. I still look forward to picking wild raspberries today with as much relish as I did years ago when I was a girl. And I must admit, raspberries are still my favorite summer treat. Not only wonderful tasting—but the very thing that good memories are made of.

On a hot summer day, nothing quenches the thirst better than an icy tall glass of raspberry frizzle. This homemade "pop" comes from a very old recipe handed down to Grandmother from her mother. It's not only an exceptionally pretty drink and great tasting as well, the really nice thing is that you can easily control the sweetness in your drink by adjusting the amount of syrup per glass.

To make raspberry syrup, sprinkle fresh-picked, washed raspberries generously with white sugar and let stand overnight at room temperature. The sugar will draw the flavor out of the berries. In the morning, take a hand masher and crush the berries until all the pulp is off the seeds. Run the berries through a sieve or cheesecloth. Discard the seeds. Birds like them so you might mix them in with your bird feeder seeds. Measure the juice. To each cup of juice, add two cups of sugar. Stir well. Heat to boiling and simmer about five minutes. Bottle in sterilized jars. Grandmother stored hers in the root cellar. I refrigerate mine.

Raspberry frizzle

To make raspberry frizzle, pour water over ice in a tall glass. Stir in a spoon or two of raspberry syrup—the drink should be pleasantly rosy in color. Add a dab (half a teaspoon of white vinegar) to the drink. If you'd rather, you can use a squeeze of lemon instead of vinegar. Stir and serve.

Raspberry syrup is also delicious stirred into a glass of cold milk, poured on top of pudding, cake, or ice-cream, or mixed with soda. For toasting special occasions, I use Grandmother's traditional old recipe for making a light, refreshing cocktail. Pour white wine into small stemmed glasses and flavor with raspberry syrup. This is a lovely drink to accompany a bunch of grapes and a plate of mild cheese at afternoon get-togethers.

Nothing tastes better on fresh bread or biscuits than homemade raspberry jam. This old recipe of Grandmother's follows her simple "rule of thumb" for jam making— "Equal parts fruit to equal parts sugar with a squeeze of lemon to 'pucker' and your jam will never fail...." Even the novice jam maker can have success with this recipe.

Easy raspberry jam

> 6 cups fresh wild raspberries (the store-bought kind will do, but honestly, they don't measure up to the little wild treasures)
> 6 cups white sugar
> juice of 2 lemons

Harvesting the Wild—gathering and using food from nature

Combine berries and sugar in a big, heavy bottomed kettle. Place over heat and stir constantly, bringing to a boil. Boil for 30 minutes, stirring and watching so it doesn't scorch. Add lemon juice. Boil to jellying stage—when a drop of jam sets on a cold plate. Pour into hot, sterilized jars. Seal with paraffin wax. Store in cellar or fridge. Makes about 8 or 9 jelly jars. Recipe can easily be halved or doubled.

Aunt Aleta's blue ribbon dumplings

Simmer for about 5 minutes:

> 2 cups raspberries
> ½ cup water
> 1 cup honey
> 3 tsp. cornstarch
> ¼ cup water

Mix 3 teaspoons of cornstarch with ¼ cup of water. Add to berries and thicken over low heat. Set aside and make dumplings.

Dumplings:

> 1 ½ cups flour
> 1 Tbsp. baking powder
> pinch salt
> ¾ cup milk
> pinch of nutmeg

Mix flour, baking powder, and salt. Stir in milk and nutmeg. Drop by spoonful into a kettle of simmering water. Cover and cook for 10 minutes. Spoon out of water, drain, and place into dessert dishes. Smother with the prepared raspberries and crown with fresh cream, if you like. These are equally good served warm or cold.

Grandmother's raspberry-buttermilk pot

This recipe I share from memory as Grandmother never had it written down. You just take some fresh buttermilk and gently heat it to boiling. Add honey to taste. Next, mix in some crushed raspberries, seeds and all. Stir. Eat hot with the help of a spoon. This is a very different treat—I find it pleasantly reminiscent of yogurt. You might call it a hot fruit soup.

Wild raspberry tea

All summer long, I enjoy a wonderful tea steeped up from fresh raspberry leaves. To make raspberry tea from fresh leaves, just pick a handful of leaves, wash under cold running water, and put into a teapot. Pour boiling water over leaves and allow to steep until desired strength is reached. If you like strong brew, use more leaves. If you prefer weaker tea, use less.

Sweeten this delicate tea with honey if you wish. To savor raspberry tea all year long, collect as many leaves as you can, wash, pat dry, and spread on screens or paper and allow to dry in the attic or warm place until crispy. Crush with hands and store in tea tins. Use as you would any loose tea. Raspberry tea is said to be a good relaxant. I find it's a nice tea to drink before bedtime as it is so mild and pleasing.

Wild raspberries are summertime's most wonderful offering. Don't let a season go by without sampling their sunny goodness. Δ

Harvesting the Wild—gathering and using food from nature

Harvesting the wild: Blueberries

By Jackie Clay

F ew wild fruits are abundant over such a wide area as is the blueberry. Found all across most of the U.S, Canada, and Alaska, the blueberry is truly a delight to gatherers of wild foods. In areas where it does not grow, its cousin, the huckleberry, grows in abundance.

The blueberry and huckleberry are in the same family, *Ericaceae*. The low-bush blueberry is *Vaccinium augustifolium*, and the high-bush blueberry, *Vaccinium corybosum*. The black huckleberry is *Gaylussacia baccata*, and the dangleberry (also a huckleberry), *Gaylussicia frondosa*.

Luckily, the blueberry is quite easy for the beginner to identify in the wild, as very few non-edibles look anything like it. But, of course, to be absolutely safe a person should go blueberry picking with a knowledgeable person the first time.

The blueberry is a shrubby, woody-stemmed plant with oval leaves. Most varieties of wild blueberry are the short, low-bush or swamp blueberry, but one of the most wonderful blueberry harvests I've ever had in my life was a huge patch of bushes four feet tall, the wonderful high-bush blueberry. The flowers are little bells, light to dark pink, hanging in clusters along the stems of the plant. Later on, you can tell the ripening green blueberries because of their little "crown" on the blossom end of the berry. When the berries are ripe, they appear a nice bright blue, but if you rub the blue dust off, they shine a deep bluish purple. Inside are several small seeds, scarcely noticeable. Huckleberries have seeds which are just a little larger.

Squeeze a berry, then sniff it. It will have a distinct "blueberry" fragrance. Then pop one into your mouth and taste. There is no mistaking the delightful flavor of a wild blueberry. They make those $3 a half-pint giant berries at the store taste positively bland. The wild blueberry may be small, but it is delectable.

Back in the thumb of Michigan, when I was a new homesteader many years back, I was telling an older woman in a local feed mill that I was canning blueberries I'd found in the woods up north the last weekend. She smiled a knowing smile and told me that I didn't have to go way up north for blueberries. She looked around quickly, then leaned close, giving me intimate directions to her favorite patch that she had picked for 30 years.

"I'm too old to go out there now," she said, "but I'll bet you'll just *love* this spot!" She patted my arm and turned out the door.

Well it was only two hours later when I drove my old Chevy up that dirt two-track in the woods, turned left at the old burnt stump, and followed a trail so faint that young trees grew in the middle. Then it ended, just as my new friend had said it would, and I knew I was at the right place. "Just go downhill from the turnaround," she had said, "and you'll be right in amongst them."

I had brought a small pail and an old blue water bath canner. Perhaps I was a bit over optimistic, as it held four and a half gallons, but she was adamant that I would need a *big* kettle. Down, downhill I walked, ending in a soft moss bed a foot deep. That in itself would have been wonderful, but glancing around, I saw huge old blueberry bushes, just hanging down with literally tons of fruit.

Plopping down on that soft, dry moss I started filling my little pail, milking clusters of the blue-black fruit off the drooping branches, the pail filled in less than fifteen minutes. My canning kettle was *not* too much. In fact, I filled that and went home to can them up. Hardly sleeping, dreaming, smelling, and feeling blueberries, I couldn't wait to go back for the next batch. That time, I took two canning kettles and a big turkey roasting pan. Both were filled to overflowing that day and two days after that. At night, I put them up as blueberry syrup, jam, and canned blueberries. What fun.

Not only did I spend hours out in the woods enjoying the birdsong, whisper of wind in the pines and oaks, but I brought home wonderful wild fruit and a memory that will last forever.

Where to find wild blueberries

Blueberries like disturbed areas, loving sunlight and a place to spread out. You will often find them following a fire or logging operation. They especially favor a clear-cut logging area.

The blueberry plant loves acid soil, so look for it where you find moss growing on the ground and strawberry plants in abundance.

I've found most of the best patches on sandy or gravel hillsides near low areas or woods. High bush blueberries seem to like their feet a little damper, favoring the edges of sphagnum bogs.

Aside from just asking around for blueberry picking spots, a good bet is to go in and talk to the Department of Natural Resources folks. Not all of them get into the woods, but they might be able to steer you to the right person. (Don't expect anyone to divulge their best spots, though. You'll just have to get lucky, or find your own picking heaven through walking many hours through the woods before season.)

Generally, blueberries begin to ripen in June, hit their peak in July, and struggle on until frost. Of course, this depends much on the growing season each year and the amount of rainfall. Sometimes a hard late frost or hail storm kills the blossoms, resulting in a poor picking in one area.

A self-reliance guide from Backwoods Home Magazine

Wild blueberry picking tips

Unfortunately, the season in which wild blueberries are the best, the bugs are too. Ticks, chiggers, biting flies, mosquitoes, and yellow jackets also are foraging. And they seem to love berry pickers. I've found that by wearing long socks and tying my jeans shut around my ankles I don't receive so many "lower bugs'" such as ticks. I also wear long sleeves to protect my arms and a baseball hat to keep the deer flies out of my hair. By picking early in the morning, you can generally avoid most of the undesirable critters that want to snack on you.

If they are really bad, you can rub some repellent containing DEET on your cuffs and the back of your hat, including your hair. I don't recommend taking it to the field, as it is not something you'd want to use liberally. I always wash my hands well after applying it, before picking berries my family will be eating. You can also use a spray repellant that your hands do not have to touch at all.

In locales where you could run into poisonous snakes, it's a good idea to carry a walking stick and rustle around in the bushes where you plan on walking and picking. Most snakes are happy to leave when they are disturbed and you can see or hear them on the move. A rattler will usually buzz when annoyed in this way, letting you know you might want to go elsewhere to pick. I've gardened and picked berries in snake country many years, and have never yet run into a poisonous snake, but it could happen, and it is wise to be a bit cautious. Don't walk quickly through heavy bush and don't just plop down where the berries are thick. Go slow and be cautious. You'll enjoy your berrying much more that way.

Then there are the bears. Everybody asks me if I run into bears in the blueberries. Of course, bears are master wild foragers. They have to be, in order to survive. (I'd hate to weigh over 300 pounds and depend on eating blueberries to make a living.) I've often picked where I've seen sign (scat and tracks) and even bears, themselves.

But they're busy snacking and really don't pay much attention to you, as long as you are a respectful distance away. I've picked on one side of a large berry patch and had a bear filling his belly basket on the other. He paid me no more mind than if I'd been a grouse or deer.

In grizzly country (Alaska, western Canada, mountainous Montana, or Wyoming) it's a good idea to be more cautious than where you would only come across a more timid black bear in the berry patch. Grizzlies are more territorial and can be aggressive. Make a bit of noise when approaching a berry patch, then scout it out for bear sign before you begin to pick. If you see torn up ground, large piles of bear dung, and large bear tracks with the claws digging into the ground away from the toe prints, you're probably poaching in a grizz's berry patch and it would be wise to forage elsewhere.

Blueberries often grow in clusters like grapes.

It's also a good idea to pick in a group. More human scent and noise keeps a grizzly away in most cases. Most folks I know out west have never even seen a grizzly in all the years they have picked berries.

The picking itself is simple. As the berries hang in clusters, one just has to milk them off by rolling them between the thumb and fingers lightly, letting the ripe ones drop into a pan or small bucket. I recommend picking in a fairly small container and then dumping it into a larger one when it is full. I've never known any berry picker who hasn't, at some time or another, dumped their picking bucket. And it's just about impossible to pick up all those spilled berries from the bushes and litter of the patch. It's a sad feeling, but much sadder if you just dumped a three gallon bucket.

Luckily, blueberry bushes do not have thorns, so picking is painless. I usually find a good spot and either sit or kneel and pick, pick, pick. It's sometimes tempting to look over a patch you are picking and see "over there" better berries. But when you go "over there" you always look around and see still a better spot. You can waste a lot of time jumping all over the place instead of methodically picking berries.

If you are patient, you can fill up a five-quart ice cream bucket in no time. And that's a lot of blueberry muffins, pancakes, jam, and pies. I try to only pick as many berries as I can put up in a day or two. Although blueberries do not squash, as do strawberries and raspberries, they are best preserved in good, fresh condition. And talk about easy to preserve for months to come. The blueberry is one of the easiest to put up and one of the most versatile. Unlike some wild fruits, there is no pit, no coarse seeds to deal with, and no peel to remove.

The only preparation to preserving blueberries is cleaning them of leaves, twigs, etc. An easy way I've found is to get an old window screen and prop up one end high enough that berries roll down to the bottom fairly easily. Under the bottom of the screen, place a large container, such as a turkey roaster. Then simply trickle the berries out of a pail. The leaves and other debris do not roll and hang up on the screen, while the berries roll to the bottom and fall into the

Black bears love blueberries, but will do you no harm when treated with respect.

pan. A friend of mine uses a towel in the same way. When there is an accumulation of debris, simply turn the screen over or shake the towel out and replace it for the next run of berries.

When they are relatively clean, rinse them in cold water, letting them bob and float about. Any remaining debris or insects can easily be picked out of the water they are in. Strain the berries dry, then pour them out in a single layer on a large cookie sheet or other shallow, large container. Go over the berries, looking for any that are shriveled, rotten, or green. That's it. You're done with the preparation and are ready to preserve your berries.

Dehydrating wild blueberries

Dehydrating wild blueberries is as simple as it gets. Because they are so small, you only have to lay them out in a single layer on cookie sheets in a gas oven with only the pilot light on or any other quite warm, dry spot. I've even used the back of our Suburban. Of course, I now also have a dehydrator that I use in the evenings while I work on the computer. A few hours, even once in a while, will easily dehydrate our lovely blueberries. It's a good idea to use a spatula and turn them about a time or two, when using a cookie sheet. On a window screen or dehydrator tray, there is adequate air flow and turning is not necessary.

You want your berries dried down to little hard blueberry "raisins." When dry, you can pour them into a glass jar with an airtight seal. They will keep this way nearly forever. The only enemies of dehydrated blueberries are moisture, which causes mold and insects, or rodents which will eat them. (Hmmmm, maybe I'd better include my son, David, as *he* eats them out of the jar for a snack.)

Home canning wild blueberries

Canning your wild blueberries is also as easy as it gets. They are high acid, as is all fruit, so you only have to use a water bath canner, processing them for a short time. Here's how. Simply pour your blueberries into a large kettle with just enough water to float them. Add enough sugar to taste. This can be very little or a lot, depending on your taste and needs. Heat to boiling, stirring well to mix the sugar in with the water. Don't boil long or the berries will soften. Dip out the berries and fill canning jars to within half an inch of the top of the jar. I use many, many half pint and smaller jars because I find that these small jars come in very handy for adding to my favorite batches of muffins or pancakes or else mixing with other berries for mixed berry recipes.

Fill the jar to within half an inch of the top of the jar with the hot syrup in which the berries were heated. Wipe the rim of the jar clean and place a hot, previously boiled lid on the jar and screw down the ring firmly tight. Place jars in hot water bath canner. Make sure the hot water covers the top of the jars by at least an inch to ensure even heating. Process pints or smaller jars for 15 minutes, starting timing when the kettle reaches a rolling boil. You can use quart jars to can blueberries, processing them for 25 minutes. The quarts make a good pie or nice dessert.

Blueberry jam

When you put up blueberries, you can scarcely make enough blueberry jam. It is one of the very best jams of all. And it is very quick and easy to do, too.

The simple, old-fashioned method of making blueberry jam is to measure out equal portions, by volume, of berries and sugar into a heavy, non-aluminum kettle that is large enough to let the jam boil while thickening. And this is much higher than you'd imagine. Pour in the berries, and then add an equal amount of sugar. With a potato masher, mash the berries to create juice, stirring in the sugar, and turn up the heat. Stirring constantly, boil the jam down, watching it as it thickens. When it is thick enough, pour it into sterilized pint jars to within a quarter inch of the top. Wipe the rim of the jar clean, place a hot, previously boiled lid in place and screw down the ring firmly tight. Process in a hot water bath for 10 minutes.

Once in awhile, the jam does not set. Usually this is because you didn't wait long enough for the batch to thicken properly. This is not a problem. You have just made great blueberry pancake and ice cream syrup.

You can also make blueberry jam with less sugar, using one of the commercial pectin products available in the home canning section of your local store.

Using wild blueberries

Of course, the best way to use wild blueberries is just to eat handfuls right out of the sun-warmed patch, with the morning dew clinging to them. But there are so many other uses for blueberries. This is the main reason we try to pick lots and lots of them.

Here are a few recipes and ideas for you to start with.

Fresh blueberry cobbler

½ cup sugar
1 Tbsp. cornstarch
4 cups blueberries
1 tsp. lemon juice
1 cup flour
1 Tbsp. sugar
1½ tsp. baking powder
½ tsp. salt
3 Tbsp. shortening
½ cup milk

Heat oven to 400° F. Blend ½ cup sugar and the cornstarch in a saucepan. Stir in the blueberries and lemon juice. Cook, stirring constantly until it thickens. Boil one minute. Pour into an ungreased 2-quart casserole. Set aside.

To prepare biscuit topping, measure flour, 1 Tbsp. sugar, the baking powder, and salt into a bowl. Cut in the shortening and add the milk. Drop dough by spoonfuls onto the hot fruit. Bake uncovered for 25 to

30 minutes or until the biscuit topping is golden brown. Serve warm with whipped cream. I usually reserve a handful of fresh berries to toss on top of the whipped cream.

Blueberry pancakes

3 cups flour
3 Tbsp. sugar
3 tsp. baking powder
pinch of salt
3 eggs
3 cups milk
large handful dehydrated blueberries or 1 cup of fresh or canned berries

Mix the flour, sugar, baking powder and salt. Beat egg yolks with milk and add to dry mixture. Whip the egg whites until stiff and fold in to the batter. Add the blueberries (drained if canned). Bake or fry on hot griddle by large spoonfuls. These are great with fresh blueberry syrup.

No time to make "from-scratch" pancakes? Toss your blueberries into your favorite batter from a mix. They're not the same, but are pretty darned good.

Fresh blueberry syrup

1 cup fresh blueberries
1 cup water
2½ cups white sugar
2 cups light corn syrup

Simmer fresh blueberries in 1 cup of water. When they are soft, add the other ingredients and bring to a boil. Simmer just long enough to blend the flavors. Serve warm over a fresh batch of blueberry pancakes and you'll earn raves, or pour this over your favorite homemade ice cream.

Blueberry muffins

> 1 egg
> ¾ cup milk
> ¼ cup vegetable oil
> 2 cups flour
> 1/3 cup sugar
> 3 tsp. baking powder
> 1 tsp. salt
> 1 cup fresh, drained canned, or ¼ cup dehydrated blueberries

Grease the bottoms of muffin tins. Beat the egg, milk, and oil together. Stir in the dry ingredients. Do not overmix. Fold in blueberries. Fill the muffin cups half full. Bake at 350° F until the muffins are golden brown. Immediately remove from the pan. You can dip the tops in butter and sprinkle sugar and cinnamon over them for a fancier muffin. Serve hot with homemade butter.

Blueberry yogurt

Simply add blueberries and as much (or as little) sugar to your favorite vanilla or plain yogurt as you want, or make a parfait by dipping some fresh blueberries into a cup, adding a layer of yogurt, then more berries on top. Top with a swirl of yogurt and a few fresh blueberries for an easy, fancy snack or desert. Or sprinkle with granola and layer in fresh strawberries, too, and you have a golden arches treat at home, without the chemicals and 100 percent fresh.

Blueberry pie

> For a double pie crust:
> 3 cups flour
> 1 tsp. salt
> 1½ cups cold shortening or lard
> cold water

Cut the shortening (or lard) into the flour and salt mixture until the shortening is the size of large peas. Add just enough very cold water to make a ball that sticks together without being sticky itself. Divide in half with one half being a little larger.

On a floured surface, roll out the larger ball. Do not work the dough too much or the crust will become tough. When you think it is large enough for the bottom pie crust, turn your pie pan upside down on it for measurement. There should be at least two inches all around the edges, to allow for the depth of the pan and the lip. When it is the right size, carefully roll the dough up on your rolling pin and lay it in the pan. Do the same for the top crust, only leave it on the board. Cut two slits in the top crust. I make these slits into stems of wheat, using the end of a knife to make indents on both sides of the top of the slit for the wheat berries. It lets the steam vent from the pie and looks pretty, to boot.

> The filling:
> ¼ cup water
> 2 Tbsp. cornstarch
> ¼ tsp. salt
> 1 cup sugar
> 4 cups fresh blueberries
> 3 to 4 tsp. butter to dot with

Stir the water slowly into the cornstarch, mixing as you go. Then add the salt and sugar. Before it thickens, add the berries. Cook until thickened, stirring often to prevent sticking. Cool. Pour into the cold pie crust. Dot top with the butter. Moisten the lip of bottom crust and lay on the top crust. Trim off the excess and seal by using the tines of a fork to mash the dough together all around or use the end of a table knife to make a fluted edge by shoving the dough toward the center between your thumb and first finger. Bake at 350° F until golden brown. Or you may rub butter on the top crust before baking and sprinkle with sugar and cinnamon for an extra flaky crust.

Serve warm or cool with whipped cream.

You can also use the same recipe to make tarts by cutting the pie crust around an upside down cereal bowl or mug to make the right size to tuck down into muffin cups. Then simply fill each cup and bake without a top crust. These are awesome when served hot with a dollop of whipped cream and fresh berries on top.

Taming wild blueberries

As with many wild-harvested foods, you can certainly bring home some blueberry plants to grow in your own garden. Of course, the trip into the woods at berrying time is one of the best things about picking wild blueberries, and you'll miss that if you grow your own.

Blueberries like acid soil, so you must acidify your soil unless it is already acid by nature. You can do this by adding one of the commercial garden acidifiers along your proposed blueberry row. Ask at your garden center. It is not expensive, but will have to be done each year to keep the soil pleasant for the berry bushes.

Till up the soil and remove any weeds or grass roots.

When you dig your berry bushes from the wild, be considerate. If on private property, ask the owner if you may dig a few bushes. It is not legal to dig on state or federal land, but the removal of a few bushes, dug over a large area will certainly not harm anything. (Don't tell 'em I told you that.)

With a good shovel and a cardboard box or other sturdy container, go out and carefully dig one small clump of blueberries, getting as many of the roots as possible. They are not hard to dig, as the roots are tough and fairly shallow. They are so tough that we consider them almost weeds here on our new northern Minnesota homestead, having had to pull and dig them out of our garden. Even after being tilled under five or six times, they still tried to come back.

After you've dug a clump and put them in your box, carefully sift soil and debris back into the hole and leave no trace of your digging. Then move to a different spot and dig your next bush. It's best to dig a few, then go home and plant them, without giving the roots a chance to dry out. We always think we can plant a whole bunch of plants, and end up with some being held over. Better to dig a few, plant them well, then go back another day and dig more, if needed.

Plant the clumps as deep as they grew in the wild and mulch them with three or four inches of leaves or straw. Then gently soak them in to make sure there are no air pockets in the soil around their roots.

Blueberries require no pruning and have few insect pests. Grasshoppers, though, will eat the foliage so if they're bad, sprinkle rotenone powder on the leaves to protect them from damage.

Transplanted blueberry bushes usually require at least one year to begin bearing well, so have patience. The fruit is certainly worth it. And once they start to produce, they will slowly spread and produce for a lifetime.

If you have no wild blueberries growing nearby, you can buy bushes that are "nearly wild" from many nurseries and seed companies. Just look for the smaller varieties with smaller berries for that tangy, impossible to duplicate wild blueberry taste. Good eating. Δ

Harvesting the Wild—gathering and using food from nature

Ramps: Better than garlic breath

By Ben Crookshanks

Every spring, a unique phenomenon takes place in the Appalachian hills—the digging and eating of ramps. In parts of West Virginia, Kentucky, Tennessee, and North Carolina ramps are a delicacy and eating them is a long standing tradition. I had a great-uncle who firmly believed that if he could get a good mess of ramps in the spring, he could live another year. I suppose it was true. He died one year while the ramps were being cooked. Anyway, I don't take chances; every year I always eat a few as early as possible, just to make sure.

The ramp, or "wild leek" (*Allium tricocum*), like onions and garlic, is a member of the lily family. Ramps love the shade and can be found growing in rich soil from western New England, south to Georgia, and west as far as Minnesota and Iowa. By the way, the word "Chicago" is a rendering of an Indian word for ramps.

Finding ramps

Ramps are one of the first plants to come up in the spring; they peep up out of the ground just after the winter snow melts. Snow doesn't hurt them. I remember once digging ramps with a couple of inches of snow on the ground. You locate them by the tips of the leaves sticking up above the snow.

They have a bulb similar to a green onion and two or three flat, narrow, pointed leaves 8 to 10 inches long and a couple of inches wide. By summer, the leaves are wilted and withered away. These are replaced by a long naked stem with a cluster of spokes on top. At the end of the spokes are tiny white blooms. The bloom is rich with honey and the plant is pollinated by bees. The small black seeds look like No. 6 shot.

The ramp-eating season only lasts roughly from April first through May. By that time, they start to wilt and are too strong to eat. People start to dig them as soon as they are up. Some eager, gung-ho types will go out to an area where they were the year before and dig them before they are up. At that time, they're not much more than a little bulb. I like to wait until later. That way, you get more for your effort.

The whole plant is edible either raw or cooked. Ramps have a scent and taste similar to an onion, only a bit more potent. They are enjoyed mainly in the Appalachian and Smoky Mountains. Several years ago, two West Virginians were arrested in a Cleveland park one night while they were digging ramps. A newspaper story said they were arrested for digging up a "plant with a rank odor." The police and the newspaper had no idea what it was.

The perils of ramp breath

Like onions, you can enjoy ramps for several hours after you eat them. Every time you burp, there they are. But heaven help the poor devil you come in contact with who hasn't eaten any. When they are eaten and mixed with the gastric juices, the smell is enhanced and greatly magnified.

Ramp breath can only be described as a stench of a royal order. Garlic breath can't hold a candle to it. It will almost curl the hair in your nose, and mouthwash or breath mints won't faze it. The only immunity is to have eaten some yourself. While onion or garlic breath is usually gone by the next day, ramp breath lingers on for up to two or three days, depending on the individual's metabolism. The smell also oozes out through the pores of your skin.

As with poison ivy and dogs that have been sprayed by skunks, everybody has a cure for ramp breath. An acquaintance of mine is an insurance saleslady. She is fond of ramps, but her job requires her to deal with the public face to face. Her solution is to drink two tablespoons of vinegar immediately after eating ramps. No doubt it works for her because ramp breath is one form of halitosis people will not hesitate to tell you about. It usually happens something like this: You start talking to someone and they immediately raise their eyebrows and look very uncomfortable. They take a few steps back and say, "You've been eating ramps, haven't you?" There are two types of inflection used in delivering the above question. One is a tone of disgust, conveying the impression, "You terrible person, how could you eat those awful things?" The other is a tone of envy or jealousy, as if to say, "You've had some already and I haven't."

Anyway, vinegar doesn't work for me. Since everyone's digestive system is a little different, it might work for some and not for others. After you try ramps and become hooked, you tend to get very callous. Your attitude is, "They are so good, I'll eat them and just let the world suffer." Of course this attitude can get you into trouble. Some schools will suspend a student for eating ramps. A few doctors will flatly refuse to see a patient who has eaten them.

The late Jim Comstock, colorful editor of *The West Virginia Hillbilly* and *The News-Leader*, decided one year that everyone should have the opportunity to smell a ramp. Since he

A bed of ramps growing in the woods

mailed his newspapers all over the state and points beyond, he figured the best way would be to have a chemist friend of his chemically reproduce the scent of a ramp and he would add it to the ink he used to print *The News-Leader*. One paper was enough to contaminate a whole sack of mail. The Postal Service didn't appreciate Ole Jim's humanitarian effort. They told him if he ever pulled that stunt again, he would lose his second class mailing permit. He countered by saying he was the only publisher in the country with a "...paper required by the Federal Government to smell good."

Up until Comstock's death a few years ago, *The West Virginia Hillbilly* was published in Richwood, West Virginia, "The Ramp Capital of the World." Cities in other states make the same claim. Nevertheless, Richwood is the site each spring for the "Feast of the Ransom." People from all over the United States make an annual pilgrimage to Richwood for this ramp feed. The "Feast" is held on the second weekend in April—weather and Easter permitting.

Preparing ramps

The most common way to prepare ramps is by frying (in bacon grease), either alone or with scrambled eggs, potatoes, and sausage or bacon. They can be eaten raw or cut up in a salad. Ramps are high in vitamin C and many consider them a spring tonic.

Organizations such as high school bands, churches, volunteer fire departments, and rescue squads hold ramp suppers to raise money. Traditional menus include, along with the ramps, ham, brown beans, fried potatoes, and corn bread. All washed down with another spring tonic—sassafras tea. Selling tickets is never a problem; the hard part is digging and cleaning the little buggers.

It takes about 100 bushels of uncleaned ramps to feed 1,000 people. When cleaning ramps, you first peel the skin and dirt down off the bulb and cut the skin and roots off the bottom. This gets rid of most of the dirt and crud. Still, to do the job right, they have to be washed several times. After they are cleaned, they are parboiled and frozen. On the day of the supper they are thawed and fried. Like other greens they cook down a lot. It takes about one bushel of uncleaned ramps to make one gallon ready to be frozen.

Personally, I don't like ramps cooked to death. I like to cut them up and saute them in olive oil, and before they change color, I dump in scrambled eggs. Overcooking ramps gives them a sweet taste I don't care for.

One sad note. Ramp dinners draw big crowds of people, and in election years big crowds of people draw big crowds of politicians. Oh well, you have to take the good with the bad. Δ

A self-reliance guide from BACKWOODS HOME Magazine

Wild garlic: Independent & delicious

By Alice Brantley Yeager
Photos by James O. Yeager

Early food gardening is often begun for us by Nature herself when some very useful perennial plants appear known as wild garlic (*allium canadense*). These plants come up year after year no matter how miserable weather conditions may be and they demand no special attention. They are like old friends—dependable and there when you need them.

Wild garlic has had a place in our garden ever since my Uncle Ed gave us some bulblets many years ago. The parent plants had grown in his Greenville, Texas, garden and he thought they would do well in our southwestern Arkansas plot. His reasoning was that anything that would survive in his area would surely flourish in ours.

Uncle Ed was right. We have had more wild garlic than you can shake a stick at ever since the first bulblets started multiplying, as this savory herb is among the easiest and hardiest of perennial food plants to grow. In Zone 8 wild garlic comes up very early in the year—usually in January—providing us with delicious fresh seasoning until warm weather drives it into maturity and then dormancy.

We have gradually moved the wild garlic into an untilled area of the garden where it remains undisturbed as far as cultivation goes. Plants in the oldest clumps are about the size of a lead pencil at the base, and first-year plants are much smaller.

This plant is a North American native inhabiting a wide range of territory from Canada to Florida and west to Texas. It grows about 10-18 inches high and has a fresh, onion-like flavor. Unlike some domestic garlics, it does not haunt its user for two or three days after eating it. Wild garlic is easily distinguished from wild onions, as the garlic has a flat, grass-like leaf, whereas wild onions have a quill-like leaf and are not as tall as the garlic plants. Color varies, too. Garlic has blue-green leaves, whereas wild onion plants are lighter in color—almost yellow-green. The onions, being smaller, are more tedious to clean than the garlic.

Cultivating wild garlic

Wild garlic is somewhat of a curiosity as it does not perform like its domesticated cousins. One difference is that it multiplies from bulblets that appear on top of a central stalk toward the end of the spring season. In this respect it resembles the growth habit of the Egyptian or tree onion. The stalk comes up from the middle of each plant bearing a thinly encased group of bulblets. As the tiny cargo enlarges, the paper-thin covering splits and a cluster of small bulbs is revealed.

Soon, scattered white or pale pink, star-shaped flowers are seen above the cluster and it is not unusual to see new shoots develop from the bulblets themselves if cool, moist weather continues. As the bunch of tiny bulbs grows heavier with maturity, the stalk will gently bend under the weight depositing

Wild garlic will grow in full sun or semi-shade and has a unique appearance when producing its bulblets. This is a valuable culinary plant.

77

the bulbs on the ground to await the coming of the next cool growing season. In time, bits of ground debris (dried grass, leaves, twigs, etc.) gradually cover the new bulbs giving protection from the sun.

The small bulbs may be allowed to mature on the stalks and harvested to be kept in a cool, dry place until fall planting time. When planted in rows, they would be spaced about two inches apart and covered with a thin layer of dirt. If winters are severe where you live, it might be advisable to plant your first bulbs after ground thaws in early spring and then let nature take its course. Until young plants are established, it would be well to keep rows free of weeds and grass. An organic mulch is very helpful.

There is no doubt that wild garlic is invasive. As new plants gradually take root beyond the parent plants, it may become necessary to weed them out of other rows. Discarded plants need not go to waste, however, as they may be cleaned, chopped, and frozen in airtight freezer containers or bags for later use.

Wild garlic is not fussy about soil so long as it is not overly rich and contains an ample supply of humus. I have seen the plants growing in both acid and alkaline soils. It will grow in full sun or semi-shade and is disease and insect-free. I have often found this valuable herb growing in abandoned yards and out-of-the-way places, emphasizing its survival skills.

Using wild garlic

An herb with more health benefits than wild garlic would be hard to find. Not only is it high in vitamins and minerals, but it has a history

Clusters of bulblets have just emerged from their thin protective jacket. It is through so many tiny bulbs being produced that wild garlic can "take over."

of being used for both food and medicine by Indians and early settlers alike. However wild garlic is not welcome in pastures belonging to dairy farmers, as there's no demand for garlic flavored milk or butter.

Wild garlic may be used in all dishes calling for garlic or onions. It peps up potato salad, tossed green salad, vegetable dips, omelets, and so on. Combined with butter or sour cream it makes a delicious spread. (See recipe)

When aphids make an appearance in our garden, I have found a spray made of wild garlic most effective. Take a cupful of packed, coarsely chopped leaves (or ½ cup bulblets) and place them in a blender with about 3 cups of water. Blend into fine puree and strain through loosely woven cloth to remove particles. Pour strained liquid into a clean, sprayer-type bottle and spray on infested plants during a time of day that will allow them to dry off before nightfall. You may have to spray a second time, but you won't have to worry about killing off "the good guys", harming a child, or doing in the neighbor's cat.

Once wild garlic is established, it's independent and capable of taking care of itself. Unlike many plants, it relieves the gardener of any further task except for monitoring its desire to rule the garden.

Native food plants that give so much for so little attention deserve a place in our gardens.

Sources of supply

You can find wild garlic in meadows, abandoned homesteads, pastures, railroad right of ways, semiwooded areas. (In other words, hunt for it. The outing will do you good.)

Wild garlic spread

Ingredients:

1 pound butter or oleo or sour cream
1 green wild garlic plant, cleaned and finely chopped
½ tsp. white pepper or freshly ground black pepper
½ tsp. salt (optional)

Method:

Soften the butter or oleo by letting it come to room temperature. Combine with the other ingredients until thoroughly mixed. Pack into a butter mold or bowl and refrigerate until firm. Just before serving apply a hot, wet towel to the outside of the mold to loosen the mixture and unmold it onto a serving plate.

This spread is delicious used on hot breads, baked potatoes, baked fish, and many other hot foods. Δ

Harvesting the Wild—gathering and using food from nature

Plantain

By Rick Brannan

Plantain is one of the oldest known medicinal herbs. It is listed in the *Lacnunga*, an ancient herbal text from the 9th century. It is also pictured in Brunfels's *Herbarum vivae eicones*, dated 1530. The Chinese call it Che Qian Zi, pronounced "Che Cheen Cho." This name comes from a story of a Chinese general in the Han Dynasty around 206 B.C. - 220 A.D. During one of the battles he and his soldiers were forced to retreat into the mountains with limited supplies. To complicate the situation, his soldiers became stricken with a strange illness, passing blood in their urine. Even the horses were infected.

He found the cure when his aide who tended the horses noticed that one horse had seemed to recover. He watched the horse and observed it eating a strange plant growing in the path. He ate the plant himself and also recovered. He brought the plant to the General and told him what he had found. He asked his aide where he had found the plant and he told him it was growing in the cart path. To this day the Chinese refer to it as Che Qian Zi which means, "Plant-before-cart."

Plantain is a traveler, having hitched a ride with the Europeans when they journeyed to this country and then with the settlers on their migration west. The Native Americans called it, "Englishmen's footprint" or "White man's foot" because wherever the settlers traveled, plantain sprouted to mark their trail. It now thrives in the cart paths of nearly every continent.

At first glance, plantain is not a handsome herb. The leaves, which are deeply ribbed, grow in flat rosettes along the ground. From June to September, the flowers bloom on a single stem, which stand out above the foliage giving it another, less-romantic nickname, "rat tail."

Although plantain may not be admired for its beauty, it must be respected for its tenacity. It prefers to struggle through life, growing in the choking roots of a fine lawn or pushing its way through the crack in a city sidewalk or thriving in the gravel of a sun-baked driveway. But a closer look at this nourishing, healing ally at our feet will reveal that inner beauty that lies within all of Nature's healing herbs.

There are more than 20 species of plantain throughout North America, but all of them fall into two major groups: broad-leafed (*plantago major*), and narrow-leafed (*plantago lanceolata*) from the family: *plantaginaceae*. But all can be handled and consumed the same. Be sure to gather plantain away from roadways and areas that may have been sprayed with herbicides or insecticides. A good place to gather wild herbs (weeds) is on an organic farm. They don't use chemicals and are always glad for natural ways of getting rid of weeds (wild herbs).

Like most wild herbs, plantain is a trespasser, popping up uninvited in the lawn or flower bed. A hardy perennial, it grows in profusion. So there is no need to introduce it into the garden, although it does make an interesting addition to a rock garden.

In Chinese medicine, plantain's energy is cold, clearing heat from the body. It affects the liver, spleen, and bladder. It is said to benefit urination, sharpen vision, and relieve coughs, expelling sputum and phlegm. A plantain infusion is a healthful tonic. Simply place a handful of washed leaves into two cups of boiling water. Lower the heat and let simmer for 20 minutes. Pour the liquid into a cup and enjoy. The flavor is smooth and earthy. You can add honey to taste, although I prefer it plain.

The young leaves have a slightly bitter, definite mushroom taste. They are excellent in fresh salad (see the recipe for summer plantain salad). The older, larger leaves are a bit chewy but can be diced and added to soups and stews. Loaded with nutrition, it contains mucilage, tannin, and vitamins A, C, and K. Plantain also contains minerals like copper, zinc, iron, and calcium, and other substances such as Thiamin (vitamin B_1) and pectin. Plantain is a good source of choline, which is essential as a neurotransmitter in the brain and nervous system, and as a "fat mobilizer" in the liver. In simpler terms, it's just plain good for you.

Plantago lanceolata, the narrow-leafed variety of plantain plants

Besides being nutritious, plantain has many other benefits. It is styptic which stops bleeding. Crush the dried leaves into a powder and keep in an airtight bottle in the medicine cabinet. The next time you nick yourself shaving, dab on a little plantain powder. Not only will it stop the bleeding and aid in healing, it will also keep you from showing up at work with bits of toilet paper stuck to your face.

Plantain seeds were once used commercially for birdseed. Band together ripe seed stocks in bundles of six or eight and store them in the pantry or any cool dry location until winter. Hang out a bundle next to your bird feeder. The juncos and chickadees will relish the out-of-season treat, as plantain seeds are one of their favorites.

Plantain is an effective remedy for insect stings or bites. Just crush a fresh leaf by rolling it between your palms until warm and juicy and place it directly on the wound. This remedy also brings relief from stinging nettles and minor cuts and scrapes. And plantain ointment is a necessity for any medicine cabinet, first-aid kit, or backpack. We use it to relieve the itch of mosquito bites and soothe the pain of bee stings, stinging nettles, poison ivy, and sunburns. The *New England Journal of Medicine* reported that a poultice made from plantain leaves controls the itching of poison ivy. It is also good for dry skin conditions such as eczema and psoriasis.

Plantain ointment

To make plantain ointment:

1. Place the contents of a 13-ounce container of petroleum jelly into a stainless steel or enamel saucepan and heat until melted. (Be sure to save the container to be reused later.)
2. Add a large handful of fresh, washed leaves. The hot petroleum jelly will foam up as it boils away the moisture in the leaves. If it starts to boil over just remove the pan from the heat momentarily. When the foaming stops and the petroleum turns clear, lower the heat and simmer for 10 to 15 minutes.
3. While still warm but not hot, strain contents back into the empty petroleum jelly container.
4. Let cool, cover and label. Use as needed.

Plantain facial

Plantain is a cleansing herb. A plantain facial is a relaxing way to unwind after a day of pulling plantain from your lawn and flower beds.

To make a plantain facial:

1. Boil fresh or dried leaves until soft. 1 cup of fresh or ½ cup of dried will do.
2. Drain and mash into a pulp. (Be sure to save the liquid. It can be stored in an airtight jar in the refrigerator for up to three days. Use it to dab on insect bites or stings or drink as a cleansing tonic.)

Harvesting the Wild—gathering and using food from nature

3. Mix the herb thoroughly with plain yogurt until a thick paste consistency has been obtained. A blender works well for this.
4. Cleanse the face thoroughly and pat dry.
5. Apply the paste directly onto the skin, avoiding the eyes and mouth.
6. Cover the eyes with a cold compress or cold cucumber slices, and relax for about 15 or 20 minutes to scented candles and your favorite music.
7. Remove with warm water and finish with a splash of cold water to close the pores and leave the skin feeling fresh.

Summer plantain salad

The plantain leaves can make a nice summer salad.

Ingredients:

```
2 cups young plantain leaves
2 cups dandelion leaves
¼ sliced onion (cut slices in half to create pearly half-moons)
½ cup croutons
½ cup cooked, chopped chicken breast
2 hard-boiled eggs
```

1. Wash leaves; toss with onion.
2. Add croutons and chicken. Adorn with egg slices.
3. Dress with your favorite salad dressing and top it with fresh grated Parmesan cheese and cracked pepper to taste. Serves six. Δ

A self-reliance guide from Backwoods Home Magazine

Harvesting the wild: Cactus

By Jackie Clay

The day was hot and typically sunny. I was hiking through Mills Canyon with a friend from town. Mills Canyon is a mini-Grand Canyon located in northeastern New Mexico's high plains. Carved through centuries of tan and red rock by the frequently raging Canadian River, this wild and gorgeous canyon bottom is an explorer's paradise. The eagles soar overhead, while the cactus bloom and flourish below.

We'd hiked most of the morning and were packing light, figuring to eat off the land. I'd been there before. We were getting a bit hungry and decided it was about time to eat lunch.

Grumbling, my friend looked around and said, "Eat? All there is around here is rocks and cactus!"

I smiled and handed her a bit of fish line from my pocket and tied on a small hook.

"Go catch a few grasshoppers and pull a few fish out of the river," I said. "I'll get the vegetables and dessert."

By the time she returned with three small sunfish, I had the vegetables frying in the pan and cleaned fruit waiting for us. There was even sweetened drink sparkling in our cups.

Knowing better than to ask, she quickly cleaned the fish and added them to the frying pan. "What's that?" she asked.

"Wild onions and nopales (pronounced *no-pall'-es*)."

"Nopales? What's that?"

"Cactus pads," I smiled, stirring them with a clean twig. "And we're having cactus fruit for dessert and cactus 'Kool-Aid' to drink."

We did, and even my friend had to admit we ate well.

Rocks and cactus? It's sad that today's person cannot see the grand possibilities right at their feet.

My family gathers cactus products regularly, and with as much enthusiasm as when we gather other tasty wild foods. I even can cactus foods for later use. They may be prickly, but they sure are bountiful and good.

Common edible cactus

The most commonly used cactus is the **prickly pear**, which grows in the South, throughout the Southwest, in California, and in the north from Oregon to Michigan. It is so prolific that it is thought to be a nuisance in many areas. But it is a great food plant.

Many Native American tribes used—still use, today—this wild vegetable and fruit. After all, it tastes good, requires no cultivation or care, and is highly nutritious.

This flat-padded, low-growing cactus produces tender, relatively spineless, bright green new pads each spring. Harvested, these are "nopales" or "nopalitos" (pronounced *no-pall-ee'-tohs*) to Southwestern and Mexican peoples. Nopalitos are de-spined and sliced green-bean size and fried, boiled, or even pickled. Bob, my picky-eater husband, ate them at every chance and said they tasted like tender green beans. I even canned them, especially for him, as they are very beneficial for diabetics.

Besides tasty nopalitos, prickly pears produce a bright red fruit or "tuna" in the fall. These range in size from thumb sized to palm sized, depending on the variety, growing conditions, and location. Prickly pear fruits are naturally very sweet, tasting like a combination of kiwi and strawberry—and just as juicy, too. One "mother" plant will produce several dozen tunas, so harvesting is quick and easy.

The only downside is that the fruits' meat is relatively thin, surrounding many large, hard seeds.

Another common pest cactus is the **cholla** (pronounced

Prickly pear in fruit

choy'-ah). This is a large, shrub-type cactus with many jointed, small arms. At first glance, it looks like a large shrub or small tree. In some areas there are forests of cholla that go on for miles.

You must be careful about the cholla, as its spines are many, and it's easy to bang your arm against and get nailed by a joint of spined cactus. Thus, the name "jumping cactus." It seems to jump out and grab you.

But in the spring, this lovely wild food producer puts out large, tender buds, prior to bursting out into gorgeous purple bloom. And these tight, fat buds are wonderful wild vegetables. Relatively spine-free, they are tender and easily harvested. I even used to dehydrate bags full, to rehydrate later for winter use. This is the native traditional use of this so-called pest. And these buds are truly delectable.

The cholla is most common in the desert Southwest, growing a bit further northward into some parts of Nevada and Colorado.

Another commonly used cactus is the **giant saguaro** (pronounced *sah-wahr'-oh*). This huge cactus, growing as high as a house with its many large arms reaching to the sky, has become a symbol of the Southwestern desert. (How many John Wayne movies have you seen without a saguaro background?)

This giant produces very large, very tasty tunas. Like the prickly pear, the saguaro fruits are bountiful and extremely tasty. Bob used to run the Arizona desert with Apache families, gathering these wild fruits, which the women would make into fruit leather and candy for "good boys" who helped.

In addition to these most commonly harvested cactus, the fruit of **organ-pipe** and **barrel cactus** provides extra dessert sweets. Naturally.

Harvesting cactus

The traditional method of harvesting prickly pear nopalitos is to pluck them with a green willow stick, folded double, like a pair of tongs. The tender green pad is easily snapped from the older plant. (You can eat prickly pear pads at any time of the year, but they toughen greatly with age.)

The few spines on the pads are either brushed off with a small twig brush or the pad is singed over a small fire. I rinse the pads well at home, then go over them again, very carefully, with a jackknife—just to be sure.

The fruits of the prickly pear are harvested when they are fully ruby red in the fall. I just carefully pick them with bare hands, but you might want to use gloves, as there are tiny spines here and there on the tunas. Like the nopalitos, you may brush them off with a twig brush or singe them over a small fire, held up by green willow branch tongs.

Saguaro fruits can't usually be picked. They often grow 15 to 30 feet off the ground. And you sure don't want to shinny

Cactus fruit, or tunas. The spines were in the tough "dots" and around the crown.

up that armored trunk. So take a slim, long pole with you to harvest saguaro fruit, as do Indian harvesters. (Bob said those poles also worked great to whack naughty boys who ate more than they gather.)

Gently poke the cluster of tunas loose, then pick them off the ground as they fall. *Don't* try to catch them. They are large, *and* have scattered spines.

Cholla buds are best harvested while wearing sturdy jeans and long sleeves, as they offer some protection from inadvertent pricks. You want to harvest the buds when they are swollen and large, but not after they begin to color up purple or loosen to open. The tight, fat, succulent spring buds are the vegetable you are after.

I would suggest using gloves and a large bucket or basket to harvest the buds. Gloves might not be traditional, but Native people have learned to be very careful handling the cholla.

The buds are relatively spine free, but check them over when you get home for the occasional pricker.

Some cactus treats

Cactus fruit juice:

In late summer and during the fall, pick a basket or bucketful of purplish red tunas with tongs or bare handed, very carefully. Brush them with twig brushes or singe them to remove stickers. Cut the tough top and bottom off and slice the fruit in half. With a spoon, scoop out the pulp. Repeat until you have a large bowlful.

Mash well, then press through a screen colander to strain off the seeds. Add as much cold water as dictated by your taste; the pulp is very sweet, naturally. You can also freeze this in ice trays until just about solid, then whiz in the blender for an icy treat. Add honey to sweeten if you'd prefer a sweeter treat.

Cactus jelly:

Harvest and de-spine fruits, as with cactus juice. Prepare as above, but do not add water. I usually simmer the skins and seeds in boiling water, using just enough water to extract the extra juice and prevent

Harvesting the Wild—gathering and using food from nature

scorching—about two cups to two quarts of cactus fruit "refuse." Add the juice to the simmering pulp and bring it to a boil.

Line a colander with several thicknesses of cheesecloth and pour pulp and juice into it, with a large mixing bowl beneath to catch the clear juice. I tie it up with a stout cord and let drip overnight. In the morning, gently squeeze the jelly bag to extract more juice. Don't squeeze too hard or you'll loose clarity in your jelly.

For every three cups of juice, add one package of powdered pectin; do not double the recipe or the jelly may not jell. Bring to a boil in a large pot, stirring well. Then add 3 Tbsp. lemon juice and 3½ cups of sugar. Bring it to a boil, stirring constantly to prevent scorching. Boil one minute at a full rolling boil. Pour into hot jars, to within ½ inch of the top. Wipe the rim clean and place hot, previously boiled lids on and screw down the ring firmly tight. Process full jars in water bath canner for five minutes.

You also may simply add lemon juice and sugar to cactus fruit juice

Cactus sticker first aid

The one problem with cactus is the tiny, brittle thorns on the pads. These quickly pierce the flesh and painfully resist attempts to pull them out with traditional methods, such as fingers or tweezers. They only break off and hurt.

Quite by accident, I discovered a nearly foolproof cure. And it doesn't hurt one bit. Even the smallest child will hold still for my extraction.

Simply coat the afflicted area lightly with Shoe-Goo, a silicone caulking-type product. Then let it dry totally. Usually, this happens with a thin coat in about 25 minutes. In the meantime, eat lunch, listen to music—anything to keep from picking at the glue. When completely dry, simply pull the "bandage" of Shoe-Goo off the area, intact. Nearly every sticker will lift off, without pain.

Repeat, if necessary. Of course if you have very sensitive skin, you might want to try a small dot of Shoe-Goo, first, to make sure you won't break out. But most folks are in such pain that they want the "treatment" **now**. I haven't run across anyone who had any problem with the silicone yet, but I'm sure there's someone out there.

and boil to the jellying point, but this requires more sugar than most of us prefer to eat.

Cactus fruit leather:

Prepare the cactus fruits as above, straining out the seeds with a colander and saving juice and the seed-free pulp. Using either a cookie sheet or plastic tray of a home dehydrator, spread the pulp out about ¼-inch thick evenly on the lightly oiled cookie sheet or plastic tray. Then simply dehydrate gently until the sheet of fruit leather will peel up easily. I then turn mine and dry awhile longer so it will not easily mold. This is the old cactus "candy" of desert Indians. In the old days, the puree was simply spread evenly on a clean boulder in the sun to dry quickly.

When the sheets are leathery and not tacky, roll them up (jelly roll style) and cut into smallish pieces with a sharp knife. Store as any other fruit leather. If you plan on storing for lengthy times, they should be bagged in Zip-Lock baggies and kept in the freezer to prevent possible molding. Ours never last that long.

Cooking with nopalitos

Pick the best, tender new young prickly pear pads in the late spring. They are best after a rainy period, as they are plumper. Brush or singe off the spines. I cut the spine hubs out, as you do the eyes of a potato, just to be sure. You can tell the ones which housed spines from the more tender, new growth. The pads are then sliced, with the skin on, about green bean size and used in a wide variety of recipes. Here are a couple of ideas:

Stir-fried nopalitos with chiles

---

1 cup sliced nopalitos
1 cup sliced mushrooms
1 cup sliced roasted chiles
½ cup sliced onion
3 chopped firm ripe tomatoes, chopped
2 Tbsp. oil or shortening

Stir fry the nopalitos, mushrooms, roasted chilies (seeded, mild, thick meated), and sliced onion. When tender, add the chopped tomatoes and cook just until the tomatoes are hot, no longer.

Serve as you would a salsa, dipped up with crispy fried corn tortillas and sour cream and grated cheddar cheese, if you desire.

You'll forget you're eating cactus.

Venison stew with nopalitos

1 lb. lean venison stew meat
shortening for browning
2 medium onions, chopped
1 cup nopalitos
1½ pints tomato sauce
5 medium potatoes, diced medium
1 cup cooked sweet corn
3 long, fresh carrots, diced
1 tsp. salt
1 tsp. black, coarse ground pepper
1 tsp. medium chili powder (powdered chiles, not mixed spices)
1 Tbsp. honey

Brown the stew meat in the shortening, then add onions and continue stirring until they are transparent. Add the rest of the ingredients and simmer gently in a large, heavy pot until the meat is very tender. Cover, but add water, if necessary. Serve with hot corn bread or corn tortillas. Pretty darned good.

Using cholla buds

Cholla buds are very succulent, distinctive, and pleasant flavored. You can pick cholla buds in the spring—usually late April to mid-May, depending on the location. Higher elevations tend to bloom later. Brush off any stray spines with a twig broom. You will want to cook or process your cholla buds soon after harvesting to prevent molding or toughening. Any that you will not be cooking soon should be briefly simmered, then dried off and laid on a dehydrator tray or even a window screen in the sun to dry. (If you use the latter method, throw an old see-through curtain over them to prevent insects from walking on your food.)

The dried buds may later be rehydrated, as is, or ground finely to make a meal. This meal is often mixed with cornmeal or acorn meal in cooking.

Fried cholla buds, squash, and onions:

Simmer dried cholla buds in boiling water until tender. Dry. Slice thinly with onion and summer squash. Add spices to taste and gently fry until done. I serve mine with salsa and sour cream. It's a dandy early summer treat. You can also use fresh buds and sliced winter squash and onions, if you want. I also toss in a cup of sweet corn when the other vegetables are nearly done, for variation.

Steamed cholla buds with chiles:

In a saucepan, add two inches of water and half a pint of home canned roasted, seeded, mild red chiles (unless your family prefers hotter food). Bring the water to a simmer. Then add a smaller colander with a dozen fresh cholla buds in it. Put a top on the pot and simmer to steam the cholla buds in "chile steam" until tender. Add water, as necessary, to keep from drying out. When the buds are fork tender, serve on a plate, topped with the chilies. This is good with ranch dressing drizzled on it and a plate of hot, tender flour tortillas and refried beans. Olé!

Fried cornmeal mush with cholla

½ cup cornmeal
½ cup cholla meal
2 ⅔ cup boiling water
1 cup cold water
1 tsp. salt

Grind dehydrated cholla buds in your food mill, grain mill, or blender until fine, like coarse flour. Bring water and salt to boil in large sauce pan. Mix cornmeal, cholla bud meal, and cold water well. Add slowly to boiling water. Stir well to prevent scorching. Cook until thick, then cover and reduce heat to very low and simmer for another 10 minutes. Pour into a greased bread loaf pan and cover. Refrigerate overnight. By morning it will be firm. Turn carefully out onto a plate and slice. Fry on both sides till a nice golden brown. Serve with butter or cactus fruit jelly. Mmmmm! (Instead of refrigerating and frying it, you can eat it as a hot cereal, with butter and salt, and drizzled with cactus fruit syrup.)

Sliced fresh nopalitos may be pickled, either alone or in any mixed pickle of your choice. Nopalitos retain their firmness and don't get limp in pickles, but neither are they crisp, as are cucumber pickles. Here's a cactus pickle recipe you might like to try:

Pickled nopalitos

---
4 lbs. de-spined, sliced fresh nopalitos
mustard seed
dill seed (if dill flavoring is desired)
garlic cloves, halved
dry red hot peppers
5 cups white vinegar
5 cups water
½ cup salt

Rinse the sliced nopalitos in cold water. Pack them into pint jars. For each pint jar, add ½ teaspoon of whole mustard seed, ½ teaspoon of dill seed (optional), 1 clove garlic, peeled and halved, a small dry red hot pepper.

Combine the vinegar, water, and salt in saucepan and heat to boiling. Pour the boiling solution over nopalitos, filling to within ½ inch of top of jar. Wipe the jar rims clean, place hot, previously boiled lids on the jars, and screw the ring down firmly tight. Process in hot a water bath for 5 minutes, counting from the time the water in the canner reaches a full rolling boil after the jars have been added. Cool. Store for at least 2 weeks to allow the flavor to develop. Refrigerate the jar before serving and serve icy cold.

Corn and nopalito salsa

1½ cups cooked sweet corn
½ cup chopped nopalitos
2 Tbsp. chopped sweet red pepper
¼ cup cooked black beans
2 Tbsp. brown sugar
½ tsp. salt
pinch black pepper
pinch turmeric
3 Tbsp. vinegar
1 seeded, chopped jalapeño (optional)

Combine all ingredients in a saucepan and mix well. Heat thoroughly. Cool and refrigerate. Serve cold. We love it on tacos and chalupas with a bit of sour cream. Remember, the nopalito is a vegetable, and can be used in any pickle recipe for mixed vegetables, sweet or sour. Δ

Birch tree syrup

By Cynthia Andal

Spring has sprung and it's sugaring-off time. For those of you who have no maples, take heart. The syrup from other deciduous trees, notably birch, though different from what we are accustomed to, is delicious.

Here in the North, though our choices of trees are extremely limited, all trees have sap of differing flavors. In the spring, this sap travels from the roots to the newly forming buds, so we could conceivably choose from any deciduous species. After some research, we chose white birch, a tree that we have in abundance.

Tree-tapping is simple and is the same for all trees. Basically you need a hole through the bark and cambium layer of the tree, a gathering receptacle, a huge fire, and a fireproof vessel for boiling down. Native Americans would slash their chosen tree, gather sap into a hollowed-out log, and deposit superheated rocks into it, thus reducing the liquid until it was an acceptable sweetness. The product was ashy but extremely valuable for trading and consumption.

Today the rules are the same:

1. The weather must be right. The temperature must be above freezing (32°F, 0°C) during the day and below freezing at night. The run lasts as long as these conditions exist and can range from a few days to

many weeks. Trees with southern exposure will run first and stop first. Because of this, tapping trees with a range of exposures can lengthen your season. The season ends when the weather no longer meets these criteria and the sap becomes cloudy.

2. We have found inexpensive metal taps, although not locally, and have found no need to make our own, although it certainly can be done. In the U.S. they are available from *Cumberland General Store* and *Lehman's Hardware* by mail order. The taps are very sturdy and with minimal care will last and last. You also need buckets, including a larger bucket to hold the sap until it is ready to be boiled down. A large, clean, plastic garbage pail does the job well.

Now, out to the forest you go, with a brace and bit (or cordless drill), a $7/16$-inch bit, the taps, a hammer, and buckets. Your chosen trees must be larger than eight inches in diameter and can hold one more tap for every extra eight inches. Thus a tree that is 24 inches across can hold up to three taps. In choosing your trees, it's important to remember that you will be hauling full buckets from the tree to the boiling-down fire.

Drill each hole 1 to 1½ inches deep at a slightly upwards angle, about three feet from the ground. Use the hammer to lightly tap an aluminum tap until it is well wedged into the tree. If the sap is running, it will be evident immediately; sap will start dripping from your spout right away. Hang the bucket on the hook and move on to tap your next tree.

The sap should be clear, cold, and almost tasteless. It is rich in trace minerals and is very healthful as a spring tonic. We and our chickens and goats enjoy this all spring. It also makes a delicious spicy tea when boiled with fresh birch twigs. Be sure you tap enough trees to enjoy all of these uses and also to make syrup.

At your boiling-down area you should have lots of firewood put up and a large shallow pot, like a wok or roaster, with lots of surface area. Place your pots filled with sap over a large fire and get them to a good rolling boil. As your level diminishes, keep adding new sap, trying to keep a lively boil in your pot. When your liquid has been reduced by half, it will be a light amber and will begin to taste sweet. Keep boiling until it becomes quite dark. This process is best done outside as it can be very messy, and the process stains walls terribly. When the syrup is nearly done, it's important to watch closely as the product scorches easily. It is sometimes wise to take this nearly finished product inside to finish on a stove, where one can more easily regulate the heat. Have hot jars and sterilized lids ready to receive the hot syrup.

The ratio of birch sap to syrup is about 70:1 (Maple is 40:1). When your syrup has reached desired sweetness and consistency, pour through several layers of cheesecloth into a smaller pot and return to a boil. Pour hot syrup into hot jars and top with hot sterilized lids. Process in a boiling water bath for 15 minutes.

The sap run ends when night temperatures remain above freezing. At this point the sap becomes cloudy and bitter. It's time to pull and clean taps and buckets and plan for garden planting, perhaps giving a thought to next year's sap run, maybe birch jelly or wine or . . .

Birch makes a lovely, very dark, rich syrup that has been likened to sorghum or molasses. Indeed, it replaces all molasses for gingerbread and other baking in our home, however its flavor is somewhat overpowering and tends to be too cloying for pancakes. Now that you've begun, don't feel limited to birch. All fruit and nut trees are said to give delicious syrup, and anything in the maple family (*Acer saccharum*) will be most acceptable. Experimentation may yield something wonderful and delicious. Variety may be the spice of your kitchen. Δ

A self-reliance guide from Backwoods Home Magazine

Harvesting the wild: Acorns

By Jackie Clay

When I was just a little girl, I used to collect acorns by the boxful as they fell in the fall. I didn't know why. They just felt nice in the hand and somehow a big bunch of them felt satisfying. Could that be because somewhere in my ancestors' time, acorns were a very important food? Native Americans all across oak-growing North and South America harvested acorns, which were nearly as important a food as corn or beans. Such tribes as the Cherokee, Apache, Pima, and Ojibwa routinely harvested and used the acorn. These Indian gatherers taught early settlers how to harvest and use acorns in their cooking, as they did corn and other traditional foods. Even today, many Native Americans gather acorns, both to use themselves and to sell in Mexican markets.

And those bright, shining round acorns are very good for you, besides tasting great.

Health benefits of acorns

Acorns have been tested and found to be possibly the best food for effectively controlling blood sugar levels. They have a low sugar content, but leave a sweetish aftertaste, making them very good in stews, as well as in breads of all types.

They are rich in complex carbohydrates, minerals, and vitamins while they are lower in fat than most other nuts. They are also a good source of fiber.

An additional benefit from eating acorns is in the gathering. Acorns, although they "fall from trees," must be picked and processed before eating, which requires a walk, then bending and picking up. All of these are good exercise. In fact, that is why many "primitive" foods are so healthy. They require exercise just to put them on the table, not just a short trip to the convenience store or fast food joint.

But acorns taste bitter!

One of the first things I learned as a little girl harvesting acorns was that they tasted awful. Unfortunately, many acorns do taste bitter. This is because they contain tannin, a bitter substance in oaks which is used to tan leather. Real pucker power here. Some varieties of acorns contain more tannin than others. They range from the Emory oak of the southwestern United States and northern Mexico, which is so mild it can be used without processing, to some black oaks with very bitter acorns, requiring lengthy processing to render edible.

Generally, the best acorns to harvest are those of the white oaks, such as the swamp oak, Oregon white oak, and burr oak, as they contain less bitter tannin. Luckily, nearly all acorns can be made usable with natural processing which renders them nutty and sweet.

From the mighty oak

Acorns are one grain that literally grows on trees. Even a small oak tree can produce a bushel or more of tasty, nutritious acorns. And that grandaddy oak out in the pasture could produce nearly a thousand pounds. Now that is a lot of eating from a small area.

There are now several varieties of grafted oak trees, which bear nearly double the harvest of wild trees. These trees are available for purchase from specialty nursery companies.

Not only are acorns great food for us, but for many birds and animals as well. Any deer hunter can tell you that one of the best spots to ambush a wily buck is on a trail to a big oak tree. Deer and wild turkeys harvest these nutritious acorns to fatten up for winter.

Early settlers must have noticed this, as they soon began to turn their hogs out into the oak woods to fatten on the bounty of acorns. I accidently had this happen to two of my own pigs. I had a litter of weaner pigs, six in number, in an outside pen. While we were in town, a stray dog came by and had great fun, chasing the little porkers around the pen. None were injured, but two of them vaulted the pen wall next to the shed and took off for the woods as fast as their little legs would run.

We hunted, called, and scoured the woods for days. Weeks. No piggies. By then, we figured a black bear, which were numerous in our woods, had a midnight snack of pork on the hoof.

Then one November, I was riding my horse down one of the wooded trails through huge old oaks, when I noticed turned-up fresh soil. Bear? Nope, my "bear" had left pig tracks. I tied my horse and scouted further, discovering seemingly acres of ground dug up underneath those bounteous oak trees. My lost piggies were found. But those tracks looked pretty big.

To make a long story short, we corralled those errant porkers and hauled them home. On putting them in the pen next to their brothers and sisters, we were shocked. Out in the woods, they really looked big, but now they looked huge. They were a third again as big. On butchering, the woods-

Nice fat, ripe acorns, ready to be used for acorn meal or flour

raised hogs weighed 290 pounds, while the grain-fed hogs barely made 200 pounds dressed. So much for "modern feeding." Of course the pigs had access to roots, grasses, insects, and more. But I credit much of their hearty size to those fat acorns they were gorging themselves upon.

As acorns hold a long time under the tree, the hogs were feasting on last year's crop all summer, then the fresh crop come fall. Not a bad natural feed.

Author grinding shelled acorns in a hand grinder

Harvesting

First of all, you'll have to check out your local oaks during the spring when the leaves and underbrush are not as dense. Get a little pocket tree book and try to identify the oaks you find. In many areas, there are several varieties of oaks available to the acorn harvester. Some are quite mild and sweet and others pretty darned bitter. If you have a choice, try to find a variety with mild meat and only a little initial tang of tannin.

You may have to simply nibble and check, come fall. Different varieties of oak have different shaped acorns. Crack a nice fat acorn with no worm hole. Examine the meat. It should be yellowish, not black and dusty (insects). Now, simply nibble and chew up a part of the nut. If it is very bitter, spit it out and try another kind of acorn. When you find a grove of relatively mild acorns, note this for next year and harvest away.

As the understory is usually very thin below a decent-sized oak tree, the acorns are quite easy to pick up. Depending on the variety of oak, your acorns will drop between late September and October, more or less, depending on your climate zone. The best way I've found to pick up acorns is to simply pick a nice dry, sunny day as soon as the acorns begin to drop and take baskets and sacks to the woods and sit down and pick them up. If you wait too long, the handy dandy squirrels and other wild critters will beat you to them, leaving only the worm-riddled hulls behind.

Processing

The term "processing" brings to mind machines and chemical additives. With acorns, processing simply means making them ready to eat.

When I get home with my bounteous haul, I spread them out a layer thick on an old sheet which I have laid on a roof, corner of the yard, or some other out-of-the-way dry, sunny place. This lets them sun dry and prevents any possible molding before I get them shelled. It will also kill any insect eggs or larvae, which might be inside. If you cannot lay the acorns out in the sun, spread them in a single layer on cookie sheets in a very slow oven for an hour.

Some acorns, such as those of the Emory oak, require no more processing than cracking them open and eating them. Like most nuts, acorns of all types benefit from toasting on a cookie sheet in an oven at 175° F. Stir to prevent scorching.

However, most acorns do contain enough tannin to make leaching this bitter substance out necessary. To do this, simply sit down and crack a big bowlful of acorns, carefully examining each nut for black holes, which indicates a worm is inside rather than a wholesome plump yellowish-beige nut. Acorns are very easy to crack. The shell is pliable and quite thin. Pop the cap off, then simply grasp it with a pair of pliers and give a squeeze. Don't mash the kernel. Simply crack the shell. Then peel it off and toss the kernel into a bowl.

When all are done, get out your food grinder. Put a fine knife on the grinder and run the shelled acorns through it. This makes a coarse meal. Place this in a large crock or glass bowl. Then add boiling water to cover and let stand an hour. Drain and throw away the brownish, unappetizing water. Repeat. Then taste the meal. It should have a bit of a bitter tang, then taste sweet as you chew a piece. Continue leaching out the tannin as long as necessary.

When the acorn meal is mild tasting, it is ready to dry. I usually lay out a piece of old white sheet in a basket and pour the wet meal on it. Then, gathering up the edges, jelly bag-style, I press and squeeze, getting out as much of the water (and tannin) as possible.

One caution—don't let wet acorn meal lie about for hours, or it will surely mold. Keep at the leaching process.

Spread the damp meal out in a shallow layer on a cookie sheet or on sheets of your dehydrator. Then begin to dry it. In the oven, you only need the pilot light or the very lowest oven setting. As it begins to dry, take your hands and very carefully crumble any chunks which hold moisture. Slowly your meal will begin to look quite good.

When the meal is completely dry, run it through a fine setting on your grain mill. The traditional method was to use a stone hand grinder (mano in the southwest) to crush the meal on a large, flat stone (metate). It is now ready for use in your recipes. If you produced more meal than you need right now, you can store the meal in the freezer or refrigerator in an airtight bag or jar. The dry, ground meal will last a week or so, stored in an airtight jar on the shelf. But, because of the oil, the meal will begin to go rancid, as will whole wheat flour and home-ground cornmeal.

You can also grind your meal in a food processor or blender a little at a time. I smile, thinking of the vast difference between grinding acorns between stones and using a food mill. What would our ancestors think?

Using acorn meal

Some Native Peoples called acorns "grain from the tree," indicating the use they had for it as a grain in cakes, breads, and thickening for stews and soups. Today folks use "cream of this and that" soups for the same thing.

I think processed acorns taste like a cross between hazelnuts and sunflower seeds, and I often include acorn meal in my multi-grain bread recipes. Adding half a cup of acorn meal to a two-loaf bread recipe and reducing the flour, as needed, works quite well. Because the acorn meal is a natural sweetener, I only use a bit of honey to feed the yeast while softening it, relying on the acorn meal to give sweetness to the bread. No complaints yet.

As acorn meal is very dense, you will have to take care to get your bread to rise when adding it. One way to ensure this is to use hot liquid and beat in your flour, making a batter. Then cool so you can add the yeast and the rest of the ingredients. This helps release wheat gluten to let the bread rise, despite heavy ingredients. Indian bread was always very dense and heavy, as there was seldom, if ever, wheat or yeast added to the recipe. It takes wheat gluten, as well as yeast, to make bread rise properly. Indian breads were often small, thin cakes baked before the fire on large, reflecting rocks. They were not puffy, large loaves as we are accustomed to today.

While camping some time, why not tuck your food grinder into your kitchen pack and try making some old-time Indian bread out of acorn meal. It really puts you in contact with past ways in a hurry. Here is an Apache recipe for acorn cakes.

Apache acorn cakes:

> 1 cup acorn meal, ground fine
> 1 cup cornmeal
> ¼ cup honey
> pinch of salt

Mix the ingredients with enough warm water to make a moist, not sticky, dough. Divide into 12 balls. Let rest, covered, for 10 minutes or so. With slightly moist hands, pat the balls down into thick tortilla-shaped breads. Bake on an ungreased cast iron griddle over campfire coals or on clean large rocks, propped up slightly before the coals. If using the stones, have them hot when you place the cakes on them. You'll have to lightly peel an edge to peek and see if they are done. They will be slightly brown. Turn them over and bake on the other side, if necessary.

These cakes were carried on journeys dry and eaten alone or with shredded meat. We cheat and add homemade butter, too. But then, we are spoiled.

Multi-grain bread with acorn meal:

Let's take a look at one of my mixed grain breads with acorn meal to see how it differs from the Indian cakes above.

```
1½ cup rolled oats
½ cup cornmeal
½ cup coarse ground, leached acorn meal
1 cup lukewarm water
2 Tbsp. dry granulated yeast
2½ cups boiling water
1 Tbsp. salt
¼ cup vegetable oil
2 eggs, beaten
About 8 cups whole wheat flour
½ cup honey
butter
```

Pour boiling water over oats, cornmeal, and acorn meal. Set aside. Dissolve the yeast in lukewarm water. In a large mixing bowl, beat the hot oatmeal mixture with the rest of the ingredients, except for the yeast and butter, adding the flour a cup at a time until you get a medium batter. Cool to lukewarm. Then add the yeast. Mix well and add enough flour until you have a spongy dough that is not sticky. Knead, adding flour if necessary to keep from being sticky. Place in a greased bowl and grease the top of dough, then cover it with a moist, warm kitchen towel and set it in a warm place until it doubles in size. Punch down, knead several times, and let rise again. Shape into loaves and place in greased bread pans or on a greased cookie sheet.

This also makes great rolls, so you can use a cake pan, making golf ball sized rolls. Cover and let rise again until almost double. Preheat the oven to 350° F and bake for about 35 minutes or until the tops are golden brown. Brush with butter and cool.

You can also make this bread in camp, using smaller loaves and a reflector oven, or by forming ½-inch thick by 1-inch wide by 8-inch long sticks and twisting the dough around a green stick and gently baking over medium coals—never a fire.

So far, we've talked about using acorn meal as a grain. But the acorn is so much more versatile. Most Native Americans and early settlers used acorn meal as either an ingredient in mush, which is sort of a thick, mealy soup, or pounded with meat, fat, and berries, making pemmican. In a survival situation which requires lightweight, high calorie foods, pemmican would be a good choice. (But, of course, many of us really don't need the extra fat in our diets.)

Here are a couple recipes for these uses of the acorn. When I say "acorn meal," I mean ground, leached-till-mild acorn meal, not raw.

Cornmeal and acorn mush:

> 4 cups water
> 1 tsp. salt
> ½ cup acorn meal, ground
> about 1 cup cornmeal

Bring salted water to a boil and sprinkle the acorn meal into the boiling water, stirring briskly with a wire or twig whisk. Then add the cornmeal. Add just enough cornmeal to make a thick, bubbling batch in which a wooden spoon will stand up fairly well. Place the saucepan in a larger container holding two inches or more of boiling water. (Use a double boiler, if you have one.) Simmer the mush until quite thick, about 45 minutes, stirring occasionally to keep it from lumping.

Cornmeal and acorn mush is very good for breakfast on a cold morning. It can be served with sweetened milk and a dab of wild fruit jam or homemade butter. But it is also great as a main course lunch or dinner. You can also add salsa or bacon bits and grated cheese on top to get great variety. This mush is very filling and will stick to your ribs.

I often make a double batch and pour the "extra" in a greased bread pan. When cooled in the fridge overnight, it becomes quite solid and can be sliced in half-inch thick slices, dipped in flour, and fried in oil, first one side, then turn and fry the other. Fried acorn and cornmeal mush is one of our absolutely favorite camp (or at-home) breakfasts. Serve it with butter, salt, and thick fruit jam or maple syrup. Of course, David likes his with catsup.

You might want to try your hand at a "modern" type of pemmican. It doesn't keep on the trail for months, but it is pretty good.

Modern pemmican:

> 1 lb. lean stewing meat, cut quite small
> ½ cup dehydrated wild plums
> ½ cup acorn meal

Boil the lean stewing meat. When it is tender, drain and allow it to dry in a bowl. Grind all of the ingredients together in a meat grinder using a fine blade. Grind again, mixing finely, distributing the ingredients very well. Place in a covered dish and refrigerate overnight. (Or you can eat right away, but like many foods, the refrigerating allows the flavors to blend nicely.) You can serve this on any flatbread, such as a tortilla.

It is best served warm, or you can reheat it in the pan in the oven like a meatloaf.

Acorn meal can also be used in place of a good portion (or all) of the nuts in most desserts, from brownies to cookies. It does depend on the variety of acorn you have available and the taste after leaching. Some acorn meal never gets "nutty," only mild, while the meal of other acorns, such as those of the Emory oak, are so sweet that you can eat them without leaching, or with very little leaching.

You will have to experiment a bit here. But the end results are usually surprising.

Oh gee! You say oak trees don't grow where you live? Well, just because they aren't "native" doesn't mean you can't plant some. No matter where I go, I always plant a big bunch of food producing trees, shrubs, and perennial plants. And a lot of them certainly aren't native to the area. Of course, you can just plant acorns or buy seedling trees from a nursery. From an acorn or small seedling, you can usually figure you'll begin to get a decent amount of acorns in about 10 years.

Want faster results? Several nurseries are carrying grafted oak varieties, meant for food production. And at least one nursery has a very good hybrid of the burr oak that produces mild acorns requiring no leaching. You can write to St Lawrence Nurseries, 325 State Hwy. 345, Potsdam, NY 13676, phone them at 315-265-6739, or find them online at www.sln.potsdam.ny.us. They have a free catalog which includes many very hardy fruits and nuts.

Oaks don't grow where we will be moving, but you can darned betcha I'll be planting them so I can enjoy those fabulous acorns. Until then, I'll just have to drive down to my son Bill's place near Oak Lake and pick a few baskets so we can enjoy all those good acorn recipes. Δ

Harvesting the wild: Hazelnuts

By Linda Gabris

While out in the woods, why not keep your eyes peeled for a tasty treat in the woodlands—wild hazelnuts. Also known as wild filberts, these little gems resemble commercial filberts except that they are somewhat smaller, their shells are a bit thicker, and their meat is so much sweeter. But best of all, they're free for the pickin' and nothin' compliments a grouse dinner more than an elegant coating of these delicious nuts.

American or beaked hazels are native shrubs which grow up to about 12 feet and can be found in abundance across North America growing in sunny spots of mixed hardwood stands. Hazelnut shrubs are often spotted hugging fences or hemming meadows.

The bark of mature plants is smooth and bright brown while immature twigs are lighter in color and covered in fuzz. The oval, double-toothed leaves have deep, well-spaced veins and are covered in silky hairs giving them a velvety feel. Immature twigs are lighter in color and covered in fuzz.

The shrubs have both male and female flowers that are separate but on the same bush. Male flowers are born in catkins, slim cylindrical flower clusters, that develop in fall and mature in spring. They dangle from bare branches shedding a shower of pollen on the female flowers that are tiny rusty clusters. In mid-autumn the nuts ripen in sets of twos, sometimes threes, snuggled in fuzzy husks that turn from green to brown as they ripen.

One of the trickiest things about harvesting wild hazelnuts is to beat squirrels to the ready nuts. If you pick them too early the nut will not be developed and you'll end up with a heap of empty shells. But if you wait too long, squirrels, who seem to know exactly when the nuts are ready, will hoard them up right under your nose. Best thing to do is hunt down a patch and keep a close eye on it. Cracking a nut with a stone will tell when they are fleshed out and prime for picking.

Make sure you throw a pair of gloves in your pack for gathering the nuts as the silvery husks are picky on the fingers.

Once home with your pickings, the nuts must be husked. If you want to use a handful of nuts immediately, peel off the husks using gloved hands. If you can wait a day or two before using, the sheaths will wilt and become easier to loosen and peel away. If you've found a good stash of nuts, they can be buried in mud for a week or two and the husks will rot off.

Hazelnuts can be cracked and eaten fresh or the kernels can be extracted from the shells and roasted in a moderate oven for about 8 minutes or until slightly brown. This gives them a sweeter, nuttier taste.

Shelled nuts should be stored in an airtight container. Unshelled nuts can be stored in a cool, dry place for years although they are so good I can't imagine a stash ever lasting that long.

If you're a huntin' nut who likes to stash away a few treats for winter then you'll love the addition of these tasty little nuts to your pantry. Δ

The enchanting Chanterelle:

Gourmet goodies free from the forest

By Devon Winter

They're prized by the world's top chefs. They're served in the most elegant restaurants. You'll pay a pretty penny for them at farmers' markets. Yet they're abundant and often free for the taking in forests all over the world. Even a newcomer can gather them easily after only a few minutes instruction.

I'm talking about Chanterelle mushrooms. You can pluck these golden gems in the hills of California or the ancient *wald* of Germany. They grow in the steamy spring woods of Missouri and the foggy fall forests of the Pacific Northwest.

The Chanterelle is distinctive and beautiful. It's a great target for novice mushroom hunters, because it's both easy to identify and rewarding to the tongue. If you become a serious Chanterelle hunter, you might even make money from your gatherings.

What is a Chanterelle?

The Chanterelle is an edible fungus of the genus *Cantharellus*. There are many Chanterelle species, but the most common and easy to identify are *C. cibarius* (the yellow Chanterelle) and *C. formosus* (the Pacific Golden Chanterelle).

These two are so much alike that only recently did scientists decide the Pacific Golden was a separate species.

The Chanterelle is lovely to look at, delicate in flavor, and goes well with "light" meats like chicken. It also makes excellent soups and appetizers. You can happily toss Chanterelles onto a fresh green salad or a pizza.

Taste a raw Chanterelle and initially you'll perceive a firm, moist, fibrous texture, but merely a slight flavor. After a moment, though, your throat will feel "peppery"—a sensation that might linger for several minutes. To me, the overall impression is almost radish-like, though the texture is softer.

When cooked, Chanterelles lose their pepperiness, but add a pleasantly delicate flavor and texture to any dish, from an omelette to a side of rice.

Where and when do you find them?

Chanterelles grow in a symbiotic relationship with living trees. They gather moisture and minerals to feed the trees, and in return, trees offer the mushrooms food in the form of photosynthesized carbohydrates.

Because of that intricate relationship, Chanterelles are almost impossible to cultivate and are not yet commercially grown (although researchers are trying).

In many parts of the world, including California and the mid-Atlantic coast, they grow around the base of oak trees. In the Pacific Northwest, they favor Douglas fir and western hemlock forests. But wherever you seek them, you'll always find them around the base of living trees.

They like mature trees. But my own personal best gathering ground has been in a 20- or 25-year-old tree farm that's overdue for thinning. They love the darkness there, the undisturbed ground, and the lack of competition from greenery.

Chanterelles are a spring or early summer crop in the southeast and many parts of California. Look for them after rainstorms in late May or June. In the forests of Saskatchewan, Chanterelles may appear in the late spring and grow throughout the summer. In the Pacific Northwest, they're a fall crop—popping up after the rainy season arrives and sharing their bounty until the first frost.

What do you look for?

Before you hunt any mushrooms, know what you're doing. If you're new, go out with an experienced person the first time.

Also, know whether it's okay to gather in a given area. In some parks, mushrooming might be forbidden. In other places, you might need a permit or an okay from a property owner. Where I live, you simply go out onto logging company lands and begin.

First, as you scan the forest floor, look for bright, wholesome gold or yellow dots near the bases of trees. Think of the most beautiful, classic golden retriever dog you've ever seen. That's the color. (And these little goldens are well worth retrieving.)

The shape of a mature Chanterelle has been described as a funnel, a goblet, or a trumpet. It does not have a separate stem and cap, but a graceful, almost seamless curve in which the stem broadens and unfurls to become the cap.

They are so goblet-like that sometimes you'll find a fully formed Chanterelle holding a shot-glass

---

Safe mushroom hunting

The old saying goes, "There are old mushroom hunters and there are bold mushroom hunters. But there are no old, bold mushroom hunters." Although yellow and golden Chanterelles are among the easiest edible fungi to identify, and although they have no deadly imitators, a first-time hunter should still think smart. Make your first hunt with a trusted, experienced person.

If you don't already know such a person, consider contacting a local club of the North American Mycological Association, an organization for amateur and professional mushroom hunters. This group has clubs all over the continent.

North American Mycological Association
6615 Tudor Ct.
Gladstone, OR 97027-1032
503-657-7358
www.namyco.org

full of rainwater. Normally, though, the top splits as it unfurls, so water runs off. The edges of mature Chanterelles are also wavy or curvy.

Immature Chanterelles appear to have a round cap, but when you pluck them and examine the underside, you'll see that it's not a true cap, but simply hasn't finished unfurling yet.

Chanterelles may be smaller than your thumb or when full grown, as large as your fist. They have a matte surface. The underside reveals fine gills, either the same color as the cap or slightly lighter, that begin below the point where the outward curve starts. The gills, the spore-producing portion of the mushroom, may be pronounced, as in *C. cibarius*. Or they may be smoother, depending on the species and the growing conditions. Wet conditions tend to produce a more pronounced gill. Tear a Chanterelle open and the flesh inside is pure white, firm, and shreds easily.

Another sure identifier: Pluck a Chanterelle and hold it to your nose. The aroma is similar to that of an apricot—the stronger the aroma, the stronger the flavor.

This photo displays the lovely trumpet-like or goblet-like form that gives the Chanterelle its name. This specimen is C. lateritius, *the smooth Chanterelle found on the east coast. Chanterelles found in Washington and Oregon usually have more pronounced gills, but they share the same basic shape and color.*

(Photo by Pamela Kaminski ~ www.pamelasmushrooms.com)

How to tell Chanterelles from similar mushrooms

In general, a Chanterelle is *not* brown, weak yellow, white, or red. There are exceptions to this rule, definitely. But when first exploring the world of Chanterelles, think *bright* gold or yellow.

A Chanterelle is *not* slick or shiny. A Chanterelle does *not* have a pointy cap, extremely deep gills, a spindly stem, or a distinct, separate cap. A Chanterelle does *not* grow directly on wood (again, there are exceptions for some rare and distinct Chanterelle species, but our little "golden retrievers" grow only in moist forest soil).

The two most common Chanterelle look-alikes are the false Chanterelle—which won't hurt you, but makes a disappointing dinner—and the Jack-O-Lantern. The Jack-O-Lantern will make you sick but won't kill you. The Jack-O-Lantern is pretty easy to distinguish, though. Its cap is more brown, it has deeper gills, and it does grow directly on wood. It's also bioluminescent—that is, it glows in the dark. A Chanterelle *never* glows in the dark.

Within 10 minutes of beginning my first Chanterelle hunt, I'd made a rule that's never led me astray: If I have to ask myself, "Is that a Chanterelle?" then it's *not* a Chanterelle. Real Chanterelles practically jump off the forest floor at you, once you know what to look for.

How to harvest

Harvesting is simple. Gently tug the mushroom out of the ground, rocking or twisting as necessary. Don't cut a chanterelle out of the ground with a knife, as this may lead to infection in the remaining stem and might damage the hidden understructure on which the next crop of mushrooms will grow.

Feel free to take both mature examples and small ones (which many people find more tasty). But don't over-harvest. Leave some small mushrooms and leave the ground as undisturbed as possible. Nature will reward you with more mushrooms in the future.

Once you've captured your golden gem, use a sharp knife to slice off the end of its stem. Then leave the end in the woods.

Place your "catch" in a basket. Carrying in a woven basket is good for the mushrooms you've picked as it helps keep them from getting mushy. But it's even better for future mushroom harvests. With each step you take, your basket sheds spores that might turn into future Chanterelle patches.

You can also tote your harvest in a paper bag lined with paper towels to absorb extra moisture. Real Chanterelle aficionados say never to use a plastic container. But in practice, people use plastic bags and buckets all the time. Just don't keep your Chanterelles in plastic very long. Empty them onto a towel once you return home.

How to clean and store

Tend to your mushrooms as soon as you get them into your kitchen. If you've sliced off the stem ends while in the woods, your cleaning job will be relatively easy. Just lightly brush off the dirt and debris with a paper towel or soft cloth. You can also use a small brush to get dirt out of the gills and curves, but you'll be scrubbing off the surface of the mushroom at the same time.

Don't wash Chanterelles unless you absolutely must—and in that case it's best to do it right before cooking.

To store fresh: Place them in a paper bag in the veggie-keeper compartment of your refrigerator. They'll be good for 7-10 days.

To freeze: Most people prefer to saute their Chanterelles before freezing. Just place a tiny bit of oil or butter in the pan, quarter the mushrooms, and stir for a few minutes over medium heat. (Chanterelles have so much moisture that with just a starter drop of oil they'll "dry saute" themselves in their own water.) You can freeze them in their cooking liquid, discard the liquid, or separate the liquid and use it in soups.

If you saute them with butter and onions before freezing, you have a ready-made appetizer or soup ingredient—just defrost, add wine or stock and spices—and *voila!*

You can freeze without sauteing, as long as you do it in small, meal-sized containers. If you use large containers, the Chanterelles' high moisture content will cause them to clump into one indivisible mass. HINT: Since chanterelles tend to get rubbery or mushy when preserved, freeze only young, firm specimens.

To can: I don't like canned mushrooms, so here I'll pass along the word of a third-party expert. According to the web site: *Wild About Mushrooms* (www.mssf.org/cookbook/chanterelle.html):

"To can Chanterelles, clean them thoroughly and cut them in big chunks and steam for 20 minutes. Place the pieces in small [sterilized] canning jars and cover them with the liquid from the steaming vessel or boiling water to make up the difference. Add ½ teaspoon salt and ½ teaspoon vinegar. Finally, sterilize them for 40 minutes in a pressure cooker at 10 pounds pressure."

You can also pickle your Chanterelles using any standard pickle recipe, adjusting the seasonings to suit the very delicate flavor of the mushroom.

To dry: Quarter your Chanterelles and lay them in the open air. Cover lightly with cheesecloth if insects are a problem. Then store them in a lidless container that allows them to breathe a bit. When it's time to serve, just soak in water for an hour or two. NOTE: Dried Chanterelles always retain a slightly leathery texture. Once dried, they might be suitable as an ingredient in a soup or stew, but not in a stand-alone mushroom dish.

A tip for dividing your Chanterelles: You can slice them with a knife, as you would any mushroom. But try this instead: Hold a Chanterelle by its top, push your thumbs into the center of the cap, and simply tear lengthwise. You can tear into pieces as large or as small as you need. Much easier and faster than slicing.

Chanterelles are extremely versatile. Here's a sampling of very easy recipes.

Chanterelle and wild rice soup

The textures of this soup are almost as good as the flavors.

> 1 Tbsp. olive oil
> 1 onion, finely chopped
> 1 pound Chanterelles, shredded
> ½ cup white wine
> 2 cups chicken or vegetable stock
> 1½ cups evaporated milk
> 1 cup cooked wild rice (or blend of brown & wild rices)
> ground black pepper to taste

Heat oil over medium heat. Add onions and mushrooms and saute. Gradually add wine. Add stock and bring to a boil. Reduce heat and simmer for 10 minutes. Add cooked rice, evaporated milk, and pepper, and simmer until heated through. Serves 4.

Beefless Chanterelle stroganoff

Here's a quick and easy recipe that will also let a preparedness buff use a few stored ingredients.

> ¾ cup beef-flavored TVP
> 1 medium onion (or equivalent in dried onion flakes)
> 3 cups Chanterelle slices
> 3 Tbsp. butter or oil
> salt and pepper to taste
> ½ tsp. basil
> a grating of nutmeg
> ¼ cup dry white wine
> 1 cup sour cream

Hydrate the TVP with boiling water and set aside. In a skillet, saute mushrooms and onion in butter. Add the salt, pepper, nutmeg, and basil. Drain any excess water from the TVP. Add the TVP to the mushroom/onion mix. When thoroughly heated, add the wine and sour cream. Heat until these final ingredients are warmed, then serve over green egg noodles. Serves 2-3.

Chanterelle casserole

Serve this as a side dish or as a sauce over chicken or pasta.

> 1 pound Chanterelles, cut in halves or quarters
> 1 onion, chopped
> ¼ cup chicken broth
> ½ cup cream
> salt and pepper to taste

Preheat oven to 350° F. Spread the mushrooms in the bottom of a baking dish. Spread the onions over them, cover the dish, and bake for 20 minutes. Remove from oven, stir, and add broth, cream, and seasonings. Bake another 15 minutes. Try not to boil the cream.

Serve garnished with fresh parsley. Serves 4.

Chanterelles and hazelnuts in Madeira

As an appetizer, this adaptation of a recipe from a famous Northwest restaurant will dazzle your taste buds. Or you can ladle it over chicken or mix it with hearty rice blends.

> 5 Tbsp. butter
> salt and pepper to taste
> 1 hearty dash of Tabasco sauce
> 1 tsp. Worcestershire sauce
> 1 tsp. green onions or dried onion flakes
> 1 Tbsp. minced garlic
> 2-3 Tbsp. hazelnuts (or pecans), finely chopped
> 2 cups Chanterelles, quartered
> ½ cup Madeira wine

On high heat, melt butter in a saucepan. While butter is melting, add salt and pepper, Tabasco, Worcestershire, onion, and garlic. Once this mixture is bubbling, saute the mushrooms and nuts. As the toasty aroma arises, gradually add the wine, still cooking on high. Cook a few more minutes until the sauce reduces slightly. Then serve garnished with fresh parsley. Serves 2.

A self-reliance guide from Backwoods Home Magazine

Chanterelle salad

Here's a quick, light summer lunch or healthy starter dish. Mix green leaf and red leaf lettuce in a bowl. Top with:

---
raw, quartered Chanterelles
raw, unsalted sunflower nuts
vine-ripened tomatoes, sliced
finely chopped slices of your favorite cheese
croutons or a sprinkling of Italian-flavored bread crumbs

Serve with oil & vinegar or a light vinaigrette dressing. Serves as many as you prepare for. Δ

Harvesting the Wild—gathering and using food from nature

Harvesting the wild: Shaggy mane mushrooms

By Jackie Clay

Most people enjoy mushrooms as an addition to their meals. Heck, I love mushrooms as the only ingredient in a meal. But most folks are hesitant to pick wild mushrooms because there are several very poisonous members of the large family. Any time a person is new to harvesting wild mushrooms, or anything else from the woodland, for that matter, it's imperative that they either accompany an experienced wild forager several times or at bare minimum, thoroughly read and take a good, illustrated field guide along with them on their first few trips.

One of the easiest wild mushrooms to identify is also one of the most tasty. How fortunate for us! This is the shaggy mane or shaggy ink cap (*Coprinus comatus*). The shaggy mane is an elongated oval cap on a longish stem, with a slight ring around it as it gets older. The cap is dry and "shingled" with light scales.

The shaggy mane is common in most parts of the country, and can occur anytime from April to freezing weather in the fall. You will often find the best picking in disturbed areas such as the sides of dirt roads, on paths, or in timber cuts.

As the shaggy mane is of the ink cap (*Coprinus*) family, the surefire method of identification is to watch for very mature members of a patch of mushrooms. The gills undergo autodigestion when they mature and quickly turn to a black "ink," which drips down onto the ground. When you see this, coupled with the other identifying features of this mushroom, you can be quite certain that you have indeed found a nice batch of shaggy manes.

This mushroom is a friendly fellow. You seldom find only one fruiting body. Instead, you will find large "streaks" of mushroom patches, often lining one or both sides of a path or road. Look not only for the more mature mushrooms, but also for the telltale cracking ground where button mushrooms are about to poke through. As they are fast emerging fungi, one day you will only see cracks, and the next day nice fat white button mushrooms.

A nice cluster of shaggy manes. Note the dry "shingles" or scales which give this mushroom its name.

This is the best state to pick shaggy mane mushrooms. I like to flick the dirt away from groups of these fat, delectable buttons and cut the whole group. If you choose larger mushrooms, be sure you don't pick the nearly mature fruits with darkening gills, or by the time you get home, you may have an autodigesting mess of black "ink" drooling on your other mushrooms.

The best way to pick these mushrooms is with a sharp knife. Simply slice the stem off at or below ground level, leaving the dirty root behind. Do be sure that the buttons you are picking show the shaggy mane characteristics as there could conceivably be a poisonous mushroom emerging among a patch of shaggy manes.

Pick your mushrooms on your way home to fix them. This type of mushroom does not hold well once picked. I usually find a patch, then go pick what I need just before dinner. If the patch is large, or if I find several nice patches, I will take enough to dehydrate. These fine flavored fungi dehydrate nicely, despite the autodigestion feature.

Dehydrating shaggy manes

Shaggy manes are easily dehydrated at home and make a wonderful addition to stews, casseroles, spaghetti sauce, and other meals. To dehydrate a batch, take the young buttons and immediately rinse them well when you get home. Let them drain on a clean dish towel and one at a time, slice about a quarter of an inch thick. I like to slice mine horizontally, to take advantage of the fleshy stem. This is a matter of personal preference. Lay them out in a single layer on a screen or on a dehydrator tray. You can either place the screen tray in a gas oven with only the pilot light on until they are dry, or in a dehydrator. They usually dry in about six to eight hours. You want them nearly crispy dry.

Once they are dry, you can store them in a wide mouth glass jar for years, that is if you can stand looking at them without using them for that long.

Cooking with shaggy manes

Shaggy mane mushrooms can be used in about any recipe that you have requiring fine flavored mushrooms. One consideration is that they are a high percentage of water, so when preparing a batch, remember that they will be much smaller cooked than they are raw. So plan accordingly. The first time I cooked up a big batch, I had scarcely enough mushrooms to give everyone a nice taste. Not enough for a hearty meal.

They can be fried, but again, remember that they do shrink. And they cause spattering in the fat as they fry, due to the water content.

One of my favorite uses is to slice the larger caps in half vertically and stuff with cream cheese mixed with either bacon bits or chives. These caps are laid out on a cookie sheet and baked in a moderate oven until done. These are *very good*, especially when the cream cheese is home made.

Another great recipe is to slice the mushrooms and lay them in a baking dish with bread crumbs and butter over them. Then grate sharp cheddar cheese over them and bake until the cheese is bubbly. Serve with fresh fried fish or a small venison roast and I guarantee you won't have leftovers.

There is one caution regarding using mushrooms of the inky cap family. Some people have a type of sensitivity to eating this mushroom and later drinking alcoholic beverages. It causes a peculiar type of intoxication. To my best knowledge, the shaggy mane has never been implicated. It has been the true inky cap, which does not have shaggy shingles. But I would be cautious, nevertheless.

Establishing your own shaggy mane colony

I have been quite successful in bringing wild shaggy manes home and "planting" them. During a damp, rainy fall period, I have carefully harvested very mature shaggy manes that were beginning to autodigest. On arriving home, I carefully laid them out in a long patch along the garden path. The next day, all were merrily running black ink into the soil. The next year I was rewarded by a patch of brand new shaggy mane buttons popping up all along the garden. And I didn't even have to arm wrestle the neighbors for my turn at this patch.

I'm sure that if you give shaggy manes a chance, they'll soon be one of your favorite wild foraged mushrooms. ∆

Wonderful wilderness wines

By Linda Gabris

From spring's first delicate blossoms to the last clinging berries of autumn, hobby winemakers can cash in on nature's bounty to rack up an exciting array of distinctive wines that'll do justice to any cellar.

I have been winemaking for years and not only have I bottled up some blue ribbon winners, but I also have accumulated a treasured stash of well-aged wines that complement any meal. Nothing makes a better toast to good health than a glass of sparkling gooseberry wine or celebrates a special occasion like a bottle of prized blueberry—fondly known by its ribbon as *Berry Blue*.

Contrary to what some folks believe, making wine is not difficult to master. Nor is it an expensive hobby to get started in. Truth is, if one enjoys being outdoors, foraging goods for the wine barrel will open up a whole new world of recreational fun. And once you've rounded up the equipment needed, you'll be delightfully surprised at what fine wines you can enjoy at so little expense.

Equipment needed

With home winemakers growing in numbers across the country it is easy to locate hobby brewing shops that carry everything you'll need.

There are huge barrels for those who purchase large amounts of commercial fruits for winemaking, but for the beginner looking at making wine from wilderness offerings that are gathered in far less quantity, the fermenting vat can be a smaller container such as a five-gallon crock or any food grade plastic bucket or tub. It's a good idea to have two or three small vats so several batches of wine can be fermenting at the same time. You'll need a large kettle. I use an open canning kettle which holds about five gallons. Add to your list some tubing for siphoning, cheesecloth, wine bottles, and corks.

Further down the road, as expertise grows, you might want to buy a fermentation jar with lock water-seal, fruit press, and corker. You'll also hear mention of strange supplements like campden tablets (stabilizer made out of sulfite powder), sterilizing powders, pectic enzymes, and other additives that can instill fear in the heart of a beginner winemaker. So I have chosen simple, old-fashioned recipes to share, ones that do not call for unfamiliar items. Historically, wines have been successfully made without the addition of chemicals, and can still be made today in the way of our forefathers. However, if you're interested in more modern techniques, talk to experts where the items are sold.

Getting started

The number one rule to top quality wine is cleanliness. All pickings must be gathered away from roadsides and other areas where they may be contaminated with herbicides and pesticides. Once home with your wilderness harvest, wash well under cold running water to remove insects, dust, and other undesirables.

Keep your equipment clean. Sterilize bottles by boiling in water for five minutes before bottling. Boil and cool water before adding to fermentation vat. The hardest part of all is allowing wine proper time to age. The biggest fault of beginner winemakers is serving their creations far too soon. It's hard to resist temptation but I assure you, when it comes to wine, time is worth the wait.

Using toast in making the wine

It does sound strange but my grandma's old wine recipes, from which I learned to make wine, and those from some Old World wine making books that I have, generally recommend sprinkling the yeast on top of a piece of toast. This was the method used in the days before "real" wine yeast was heard tell of. As far as I see, there's not much difference in the two kinds of yeast, but regular yeast is cheaper and easier to come by—especially for country folks.

The yeast is sprinkled on the toast and the toast is floated. Why? From what I figure, the toast swells up on the liquid, becoming moist and giving the yeast a base to grow on, thus prompting the "working" process. If the yeast is added directly to the juice, sometimes it will be stunted or not activate itself. It thrives on the toast.

I've heard that you can directly add the yeast to the juice and some wine makers vouch that it works. I use the toast method as I've always had luck with starting the fermenting process this way.

As for what kind of toast, it's funny because I've seen old recipes for chokecherry wine calling for whole wheat toast and other recipes, like for blackberry, asking to use white toasted bread. I generally use white, but don't think it would make much difference as the purpose is to give the yeast time to activate. As least that's how I've got it figured.

Some old recipes call for the yeast to be softened in water, then spread on the toast. I haven't tried that method but apparently it works also.

Yeast is used to prompt fermenting or working. The recipes below call for one packet (eight grams) or ¼ ounce of dry yeast. For each recipe you will need one piece of toast. To add the yeast: Place the toast on the juice in fermentation crock and sprinkle it with yeast. Even though all recipes below can be halved, doubled, or tripled, the amount of yeast will remain the same.

A bit about sugar. You can always increase sugar amounts in any recipe to produce sweeter wines. However, unless recommended, do not decrease sugar or you might end up with vinegar.

When a recipe calls for straining juice, use clean cheesecloth and be sure to twist and wring it well in order to get out all the pulp and juice before discarding skins, seeds, and pits.

Juice ferments best at room temperature. Always cover the crock with clean cloth while fermenting is taking place. After the wine is done working (bubbling has ceased), finish it off by siphoning into bottles, corking, and labeling. When siphoning, leave sediments in vat and discard. Store wine on its side in a cool, dark place.

Dandelion wine

> 4 quarts dandelion flowers
> 1 gallon water
> ½ pound chopped golden raisins (raisins can be added to any wine for extra body. Use golden raisins for white wines and dark raisins or currants for reds.)
> 2 oranges
> 1 lemon
> 4 pounds sugar
> yeast preparation

Gather dandelion flowers on a dry day when they are fully open. Remove the stalks but leave the green sepals on. Wash the flowers and put them in a large bowl. Cover with ½ gallon of boiling water. Cover with a cloth and let the flowers steep 24 hours or overnight. Pour into a kettle with raisins, grated rind, and the pulp and juice of the oranges and lemon. Bring to a boil, add the sugar, stirring until dissolved. Simmer for 30 minutes. Let cool and pour into a crock. Add ½ gallon of water, then add the yeast. Cover and let ferment for two to three weeks or until the wine stops working. Finish off by siphoning into bottles, corking, and labeling.

Billy's Blackberry wine

Wild blackberries make superb, full-bodied distinctive wine. We pick blackberries for wine from the hedges that surround our friend, Billy's, farm. Thus our blackberry bears his name. If you can't harvest from the wild, commercial blackberries are well worth the investment for this robust wine.

> 1 gallon blackberries
> 1 gallon water
> sugar (as needed—see the instructions below)
> yeast preparation

Put the berries in a bowl and cover with boiling water. Let stand 24 hours or overnight. Put in kettle, bring to boil. Simmer 10 minutes. Strain. Measure the juice. Add one cup sugar to two parts juice for dessert wine, or one part sugar to three parts juice for less sweet wine. Empty into the crock, add the yeast, and ferment for two to three weeks. Finish off. Try to resist temptation for at least nine months. This is a very fine wine.

Variation: Substitute raspberries for a lighter, red wine that has a rich fruity flavor. A mix of blackberry and raspberry can be used for a unique cellar treat.

Berry Blue wine:

I love picking blueberries and since they are so plentiful, it's easy to keep the cellar well-stocked with this full-bodied wine.

> 2 gallons blueberries
> 2 gallons water
> 2 oranges, rinds grated, pulp and juice reserved
> 6 pounds sugar
> yeast preparation

Mash the berries and set aside. Bring one gallon water to a boil. Add the sugar and prepared oranges and boil five minutes. Pour over the berries. Let stand 24 hours or overnight. Mash again. Pour into a crock. Add one gallon of water and yeast. Ferment for two to three weeks, stirring occasionally, until the wine stops working. Strain. Put back into the crock and let it settle for three days. Finish off.

Pin Cherry wine:

Pin cherries are tiny but bursting with flavor. The trick to getting enough for the crock is beating birds to trees when fruit is ripe. If you can't harvest enough for a batch of wine, make up the difference with tame cherries. Or substitute chokecherries, which are often more plentiful, for a deeper wine. And keep in mind that you can mix and match to create unique wines.

> 1 gallon pin cherries (or chokecherries)
> 2 cups chopped maraschino cherries, with juice
>   (only if using pin cherries)
> 1 gallon water
> 5 pounds sugar
> yeast preparation

Put the cherries in a kettle with one quart of water. Bring to a boil. Reduce the heat and simmer, mashing until pulpy. Remove from heat and let stand 24 hours or overnight. Strain. Put the juice in the kettle and add three quarts of water and the sugar. Bring to boil and simmer for 20 minutes. Cool. Pour into a crock and add the yeast. Ferment for two to three weeks. Finish off.

Old World Gooseberry wine

This medium-dry wine was used as an Old World curative for all kinds of common complaints. Today it's drunk for sheer pleasure. If you can't get enough gooseberries for a batch, make up the difference with wild currants, which usually grow in the same woodlands. Or tame garden gooseberries can be used. A quart of wild or tame frozen strawberries or raspberries adds pink color and flair to this delightful wine.

Harvesting the Wild—gathering and using food from nature

> 4 quarts gooseberries
> 1 pound golden raisins
> 1½ gallons water
> 4 pounds sugar
> 1 quart liquid honey
> yeast preparation

Bring water to a boil and drop in the gooseberries and raisins. Simmer an hour. Let stand 24 hours or overnight. Empty the mixture back into the kettle. Bring to a boil. Add the sugar and honey, boil five minutes. Cool. Strain juice into crock and add yeast. Ferment for two to three weeks. Finish off. Wait at least eight months—or longer if you can—before decanting. This one improves greatly with age.

Be bear aware

When foraging in the woodlands be…**bear aware**. Don't let your guard down when it comes to bears. They, too, are especially fond of berries. When you go down in the woods, don't go alone. Go in numbers. Make noise. Wear bells. Sing and be merry. If you've got a hunch there's a bear in the air, there probably is. When in doubt, leave. Slowly. Calmly. Never have a picnic in the patch or carry food in your pocket. If confronted by a startled bear, back away slowly. Don't run—bears can do over 30 miles an hour when the race is on. When a bear is spotted in the patch, do not close it in. Make your exit as unthreatening as possible. Avoid blocking or crossing its path. Δ

A self-reliance guide from Backwoods Home Magazine

Wonderful wilderness teas

By Linda Gabris

When I was a kid, one of my favorite pastimes was arming up with baskets and taking off on foot with Grandmother through the backyard woodlands in search of wonderful wilderness picks for the teapot.

Grandmother was a relied-upon herbalist in our rural neck of the woods and folks would come from miles around to seek her cures for their everyday ailments and common complaints. Since many of her medicinal concoctions were steeped from wild plants, we gathered often to keep up with demand.

I still love wild teas today as much as I did then and every season dishes up an array of fine pickings, making gathering a fun, rewarding year-round hobby. From the first tender shoots and buds of spring to the last clinging berries of winter, there's always a tantalizing pick waiting to be had.

Although Grandma kept a couple tins of imported real black and green loose tea leaves from China on her pantry shelf which she bought from a mail order catalogue and claimed were "very dear," these were not called upon nearly as often as our carefully chosen wilderness picks which were number one in Grandma's book for both pleasure drinking and for medicinal purposes. The commercial teas, Grandma would wink, were for discriminating guests who weren't adventuresome enough to "sip on the wild side."

Like Grandma, I prefer wild picks over commercial teas partly because they are so much fun to gather and partly because they are every bit as satisfying. But mostly because there is such great variety of plants to choose from and, I must admit, what could be better than the fact that you can load up your tea pantry for free!

To be politically correct, the word "tea" refers to the leaves and buds of the tea plant known as *Camellia sinensis*, which is native to Asia. There are numerous camellia species which various types of imported teas such as black, green, white, and oolong are harvested and processed from. The traditional steeped beverage made from the cured leaves of the tea plant is rightfully known as "tea."

Wild teas—infusions made from leaves and other parts of wild plants and garden herbs—are properly known as tisanes, herbal teas, or ptisan. In my book, the biggest difference between real teas and wild teas or tisanes is the fact that wild teas are caffeine-free and imported real teas are not. This is a big bonus for those who wish to avoid the stimulant drug caffeine, which causes sleeplessness, migraine headache, and other discomforts in some users.

Even though it's against the law in several tea-growing countries to use the word "tea" loosely, pardon the pun, here in North America it is acceptable to call any steeped infusion tea—whether it is made from the real camellia plant or brewed from a wild or herbal pick.

Wilderness teas can be made from fresh or dried leaves, buds, flowers, berries, bark, needles, and roots of wild plants. When making infusions for medicinal purposes, the amount of fresh or dried plant can be increased for more potent brew. Honey is my choice of sweetener as it compliments wild teas with natural goodness. Lemon can be added, if desired.

Below are some easy to identify, plentiful plants for the beginner tea forager to satisfy their thirst with. But before hitting the trail, here are a few rules to abide by. Do not harvest plants in areas where they may be contaminated with road dust, herbicides, and pesticides. Never pick a plant you can't positively identify, and do not pick scarce plants or those that are protected by law.

Individual leaves can be dried for winter use by spreading on sheets of clean cloth or paper and drying in a warm place until moisture is gone. Those gathered on the stems can be dried by tying stalks into bundles with string and hanging in an airy place until crisp and then stripping the leaves off the stalks with your hands. Label and store dried leaves in zip-lock baggies, paper bags, tea tins, or cloth sacks like Grandmother did since she didn't have access to modern day packaging.

Flowers, buds, berries, and other smaller gatherings can be dried by spreading on sheets of clean cloth or paper and drying in warm place until moisture is gone. Or they can be dried in the oven at the lowest temperature setting with the door left slightly ajar in order for moisture to escape or in a food dehydrator according to manufacturer's directions. If you have a wood stove such as the one grandmother passed down to me, you can use the warming oven for drying.

To make tea, always start with a clean preheated teapot. If using fresh plant, wash well, pat dry with paper towels, and put into pot. Cover with fresh rapidly boiling water. Since some plants taste stronger than others, you will have to adjust amounts to suit your own taste. A general rule of thumb is to use a small handful of fresh plant per pot of tea unless otherwise stated. If using dried plant, begin with 1 to 2 tablespoons per cup. Cover and steep until desired strength is reached. If making the tea for medicinal purpose, the infusion can be made more potent by increasing amount of plant and steeping longer.

In summertime, like Grandmother, I often serve wild teas, especially strawberry, raspberry, blueberry, clover, pineapple weed, and mint tea over ice. They are refreshing and help cool the body down. In winter, I

Harvesting the Wild—gathering and using food from nature

prefer my teas freshly steeped and steaming hot to warm up the body and ward off chilblains.

A tip for those who have houseplants—never waste leftover cold tea! I use it to water my houseplants and then I sprinkle the spent leaves on the soil and work it in with my fingers for nutritional boost. You will notice your plants perk up instantly from a taste of woodland wonder.

The number one reason for drinking wild teas is, of course, to enjoy the sheer pleasure of quenching your thirst with a pick from Mother Nature's pantry but as Grandma would say, why not reap the healthful benefits as a bonus deal.

So, I have included some wild tea "cures" for common discomforts as recorded in Grandmother's old handwritten doctoring journals. But do heed her stern warning and consult a doctor for expert advice when needed.

Dandelion

Dandelion is one of the most common of all plants and, no doubt, one of the most plentiful to quench your thirst with. Rich in beta carotene, dandelion is an Old World remedy for improving eyesight. It is also noted as being good for treating gout, cleansing blood, flushing impurities out of the liver, and a host of other claims including aiding the digestive system, which is why Grandma often served it with supper, to help the body handle the heaviest meal of the day. The leaves contain various vitamins as well as iron, calcium, potassium, magnesium, and zinc. They can be gathered throughout their growing season.

Raspberry tea—sweet, fragrant wild tea, good for whatever ails you.

Leftover cold dandelion tea makes a soothing wash for sunburn skin, hives, and rashes. Dandelion roots can be dug, scrubbed, and roasted for a very fine coffee substitute that is caffeine-free, a delightful drink for those who like to start their morning with a perky brew similar in taste to coffee. I don't need to tell anyone where the dandelions grow and after tasting the tantalizing tea, maybe you won't frown upon them for being such a pesky yard weed.

Strawberry, raspberry, blackberry, blueberry

Leaves and berries of these common plants make delightfully sweet fragrant teas. I gather the leaves from bountiful woodland patches before the fruits ripen and I pick in a thinning-out fashion rather than stripping the plants bare. (I also save the trimmings off my cultivated berry bushes for use as tea—but only if you grow organically as I do.) This pruning helps the plant produce more fruits, which I go back to gather when the time is right. You only need to add a small amount of dried berries to the leaves in order to greatly increase the flavor and aroma of the tea. Berry teas can be mixed and matched for tutti-frutti flavors and it is so much fun to create your own tea blends. For medicinal purposes, strawberry tea is noted as being a mild laxative, raspberry tea helps keep the body regular, blackberry tea is said to be preventive medicine for heart attacks and strokes as well as being useful treatment for sore throats, and blueberry tea is raved about as being a powerful antioxidant helping the body ward off cancers and other invaders.

Dried blueberries and leaves

Violet

When spring woodlands are loaded with violets, or when they take over my backyard wilderness garden, I cash in on one of the most delicate picks in Mother Nature's tea pantry. Since the Victorian era, violet tea has held ground as the finest of all teas for the fairest of all sippers. Like a fine wine, to enjoy the fragrance of the tea it should be served in a porcelain teacup with a low wide bowl so you can hold your face over the cup in order to savor the aroma. Grandma vouched that violet tea kept the mind young and the body agile. Violets should be gathered in the forenoon after the dew has dried but before the sun has set itself down upon the flowers, drying out the essential oils. I gather leaves along with the flowers to add a pretty tint of green to the pot. Violets grow in abundance on the rich moist floors of hardwood stands and in open fertile meadowlands. If you love the tea, sprinkle some violet seeds in a corner of your backyard and they will take root and multiply. Pansies, too, release lots of flower-power into the teapot, if you have a backyard patch to harvest from.

Mint

Whether you gather mint from your backyard garden or mint from the wilds, it makes a very comforting pot of tea—as good hot as it is cold. Grandma recommended mint tea for those suffering from heartburn, upset stomach, indigestion, gas, travel sickness, and nausea. I often follow Grandma's old advice and sip a cup of mint tea for cold and flu treatment and find that inhaling the vapor relieves headache and breaks up congestion. Mint grows wherever it takes a notion. Find a patch and you can harvest from it forever.

Stinging nettle

Stinging nettle tea is rich in minerals and vitamins and is reputed as being an Old World cure-all, especially good for flushing impurities from the body and cleansing the system. As far back as history dates, nettles have been used for everything from common ailments like cold

Stinging nettle is noted as being an Old World cure-all. Wear gloves when you pick them.

and sore throat to serious afflictions like scurvy and cancers. Modern day research is looking at nettle preparations as possible treatment for various conditions including prostate cancer and hepatitis. Look for stinging nettles in open moist woodlands from early spring onward. Wear gloves for harvesting as they do sting.

Wild rose

Wild roses are the most versatile of all woodland plants for the teapot. From the first buds of spring to the last clinging hips of winter, wild roses are readily available. Infusions made from buds and petals are the most romantic of all teas, having a delicate rose aroma. The hips from fall onward throughout the winter are a rich source of vitamin C, thus tea made from hips is excellent cold and flu cure and preventive medicine. It is the most nutritional of all woodland teas. The easiest way to dry rose hips for tea is to simply pick them by the basketful and set them in a warm place to dry, shaking the basket occasionally until all the hips are

Dried rose flowers and hips

shriveled. They are now ready for the teapot. However, if you want to eat the hips as an extra boost of energy, as I do, break them in half and thumb out the seeds and discard before drying as they contain bristly hairs that can irritate the mouth if eaten. Should you ever find yourself in a survival situation, pray tell, keep in mind that rosehips are a number one survival food since they are rich in nutrients and available year-round.

Clover flowers

This is one of my favorite wild teas and since it is so plentiful, I gather lots. Grandma sang many praises about the healing properties of clover tea, vouching it was number one cure for calming the nerves and inducing sleep. It is reputed as being a blood purifier, a deterrent to stomach cancer, flushing impurities from the body, and a general cure-all tonic. Purple, pink, red, white, and yellow clover flowers can be mixed for healthful teas that are not only wonderfully thirst quenching, but exceptionally pretty when flowers are dried and mixed together. After the teapot is emptied, eat the dregs for good measure. For a double dose of clover goodness, sweeten the tea with clover honey. Look for clovers in meadowlands, farmlands, open sunny woodlands, or wherever rich grasses grow.

Dried purple clover blossoms make a calming cup of tea.

Pineapple weed

Pineapple weed (*Matricaria discoidea*), with its pretty little cone-shaped yellow flower head and appealing chamomile-pineapple-like aroma, is one of my favorite teas. It is good for aiding digestion when it is drunk before mealtimes and can help eliminate gas from rich foods. Warm pineapple weed tea can be used as an antiseptic wash for cuts and sores and the cold tea makes a soothing gargle for sore throat. The neat thing about this plant is that you can often catch a whiff of its pungent aroma before you even land in the patch. It can thrive on poor soil and grows in abundance on waste grounds around old roads, footpaths, pasturelands, and even can be found forcing its way through the toughest, hardest soil. Bruise the plant before adding to the teapot to help release flavor and aroma.

Currant

There are various species of wild currants with fruits ranging in color from red to blue and black. Although it is often difficult to gather enough wild currants for jam and jelly making, it is easy to gather enough fruits to mix with the plentiful leaves throughout their growing season for rich, healthful teas. Gooseberries are closely related to currants so add them to your picking baskets, too. Currants serve up a healthful dose of vitamin C, thus the tea is good cold and flu medicine and excellent for soothing sore throat. Grandma recommended the tea for those suffering from rheumatism and arthritis pain and would often brew Grandpa up a pot when the weather was causing his bones to ache. Currants grow on fertile moist grounds around stream banks and swampy, low-lying woodlands. Tame currants can be used for tea, too, if you have a flourishing backyard patch.

Yarrow

I love the smell of yarrow and find that it makes a cup of tea that is good for calming the nerves and inducing sleep. Yarrow tea is a number one treatment for colds and flu and, according to Grandma's old notes, is good for the circulatory, digestive, and urinary systems as well as being a blood purifier. Drinking the cool tea relieves toothache pain and inhaling soothing yarrow vapor off steaming tea breaks up congestion and eases headache. Cold yarrow tea can be used as a cleansing wash for cuts, sores, and wounds. Since yarrow contains salicylic acid (a component of aspirin), it can be used for treating fever and reducing pain. Yarrow grows in open woodlands, edges of fields, and meadowlands.

Fragrant yarrow tea calms nerves and induces sleep.

Evergreen needle tea

Pine, spruce, balsam, and fir needles can be gathered all year round for aromatic, spicy teas. The needles are a good source of vitamin A and are rich in vitamin C, making them another useful pick for not only treating the discomforts of cold and flu but also for drinking as preventive medicine. Use about three or four sprigs of needles (with stems intact for added sweetness) per pot. Strain upon serving. Gum blisters from the tree (sap that has flowed from the tree and hardened into resinous bumps) can be added to the pot for stronger infusions when using the tea for medicinal purposes. The hardened sap, also called balsam gum, is similar in taste to the noted "it tastes awful but it works Buckley's cough syrup" and works just as well at breaking up chest cold.

Birch and maple twig

You can get a sweet cup of tea from a small handful of birch and maple twigs, especially in springtime when the sap is running. Just break off a few twigs, those with some buds are ideal, and put them in the teapot. Cover with boiling water and steep until all the goodness has been leached out of the twigs. This makes a faintly sweet and delightfully good tea. This is another pick that is well-worth remembering in a survivor situation as the sap is nourishing—in which case you would want to steep it up as strongly as possible, or even collect some of the flowing sap if possible.

Wild ginger

Wild ginger (*Asarum canadense*) is a low-lying plant that grows in abundance on fertile shady grounds in rich leaf rot of deciduous forests across North America. It is easily recognized by it "gingery" aroma, very similar to that of imported ginger root. The leaves resemble those of a "pond lily," lustrous green and very fragrant. The plant grows on a long snaking rhizome known as a snakeroot, barely beneath the surface of ground. It flowers in spring as soon as the sun hits the woodland floor. Even though the flowers are exceptionally pretty, they are often overlooked by the untrained eye because they hug the ground so closely. Wild ginger tea is useful treatment for upset stomach and insomnia, and various Indian tribes used it as cure for irregular heartbeat and poured it warm into the ear to treat earaches. Grandmother vouched it was a good system cleaner, especially if the tea was drunk in the spring. Wild ginger can be gathered from early spring until it is hidden under the winter snows. For more pungent tea, steep a small portion of fresh or dried root along with the leaves.

Dried wild ginger—Mother Nature's most pungent plant

Labrador tea

Grandma called this the "Indian tea plant." Being an evergreen, Labrador tea can be harvested all year round and according to old writings, it was often dug up in the winter to treat various ailments such as stomach disorders, weak blood, poor circulation, and tuberculosis. Grandma vouched that inhaling the steam of Labrador tea was number one treatment for sinus headache. It has very pungent smelling leaves. You will find the heartiest patches growing on peat-rich soils and mossy grounds.

Juniper

Juniper has held ground for centuries as being a cure for many complaints including flushing impurities from the system, heartburn, rheumatism and arthritis, bad circulation, bronchitis, bad breath, and even gout, or so Grandma mentions. Known in Dutch as *geniver*, it is the plant which gives gin its unique Christmas tree-like flavor and from which it got its name. The tea is also very soothing for sore throat and good for helping to break up cough. Use ½ tablespoon bruised berries per 1 cup of boiling water and steep about 5 minutes. Grandmother has it noted that pregnant women should not indulge in this tea as it was used by the North American Indians as a medicine to help induce labor. Juniper tea should be drunk in moderation as it is one of the most potent of all woodland teas. ∆

A self-reliance guide from Backwoods Home Magazine

Notes

Notes

A self-reliance guide from Backwoods Home Magazine

My favorites

My favorites

A self-reliance guide from Backwoods Home Magazine

Other titles available from *Backwoods Home Magazine*

The Best of the First Two Years
A Backwoods Home Anthology—The Third Year
A Backwoods Home Anthology—The Fourth Year
A Backwoods Home Anthology—The Fifth Year
A Backwoods Home Anthology—The Sixth Year
A Backwoods Home Anthology—The Seventh Year
A Backwoods Home Anthology—The Eighth Year
A Backwoods Home Anthology—The Ninth Year
A Backwoods Home Anthology—The Tenth Year
A Backwoods Home Anthology—The Eleventh Year
A Backwoods Home Anthology—The Twelfth Year
A Backwoods Home Anthology—The Thirteenth Year
A Backwoods Home Anthology—The Fourteenth Year
Emergency Preparedness and Survival Guide
Backwoods Home Cooking
Can America Be Saved From Stupid People
Chickens—a beginner's handbook
Starting Over—Chronicles of a Self-Reliant Woman
Dairy Goats—a beginner's handbook
Self-reliance—Recession-proof your pantry
Making a Living—Creating your own job
Growing and Canning Your Own Food
The Coming American Dictatorship—Parts I-XI